THE CONCISE GUIDE TO
HIP-HOP MUSIC

THE CONCISE GUIDE TO

HIP-HOP
MUSIC

A FRESH LOOK AT THE ART OF HIP-HOP, FROM OLD-SCHOOL BEATS TO FREESTYLE RAP

PAUL EDWARDS

🎤 ST. MARTIN'S GRIFFIN 🎵 NEW YORK

www.stmartins.com

Designed by Steven Seighman

The Library of Congress Cataloging-in-Publication Data is available upon request.

ISBN 978-1-250-03481-6 (trade paperback)
ISBN 978-1-250-03482-3 (e-book)

St. Martin's Griffin books may be purchased for educational, business, or promotional use. For information on bulk purchases, please contact the Macmillan Corporate and Premium Sales Department at 1-800-221-7945, extension 5442, or write to specialmarkets@macmillan.com.

First Edition: February 2015

10 9 8 7 6 5 4 3 2 1

Contents

Acknowledgments

Thanks to my parents, friends, family, agent, and to all the people at St. Martin's Press for making this book a reality.

Thanks to Adam "Eightzero" Wroblewski for all the help, information, input, and discussion. Thanks to all the MCs, beatmakers, and everyone else involved in hip-hop who has contributed to the art form.

Also, thanks to the writers, scholars, journalists, filmmakers, and everyone who has added to hip-hop research, knowledge, and preservation.

PART I

HIP-HOP 101

1. What Is Hip-Hop?

The term *hip-hop* made its first appearance at parties. Keith Cowboy, of the group Grandmaster Flash and the Furious Five, started using the term around 1975, and it was then adopted by other popular rappers of the time.

Kid Creole, Grandmaster Flash and the Furious Five
On that term Hip Hop. A friend of ours named Billy was about to go to the Army, I think this was '75. We had a party.... This was Billy's last weekend before shipping out, and Cowboy was on the mic playin' around doing that Army cadence: Hip/Hop/Hip/Hop. But he was doin' it to music and people was diggin' on it.... Cowboy was the first one I heard do that to music, as part of his crowd response.[1]

Grandmaster Caz, Cold Crush Brothers
Hip-hop was a word that was first coined by Keith Cowboy and made popular by Lovebug Starski. It was like a bridge between what you were saying, like you're saying a rhyme, and then you get to the end of it and you're going, "to the hip, the hop, the hip hip, the hop, it don't stop."[2]

The term was then picked up by the media covering the music at the time. Afrika Bambaataa applied the term to the entire scene, presenting the scene to members of the press as a fully formed movement.

Afrika Bambaataa

[The term *hip-hop*] was really from my brothers Love Bug Starski and Keith Cowboy, who were using it in their rhymes. So when [the media] came to ask us what to call the whole thing, I could've said the go-off, the jim-jam or whatever. But I remembered the rhymes they were doing, so I said, "We call this whole culture hip-hop." Because it was hip and you got to hop to the beat.[3]

Steven Hager

Fab 5 Freddy introduced me to Afrika Bambaataa, and Afrika Bambaataa told me that the name of the culture was *hip-hop*. That's the first time I ever heard the word *hip-hop* in my life. The first time it appears in print, as far as I know, is when I write my first article for the *Village Voice* on Afrika Bambaataa [in 1982].[4]

Hip-Hop Music

Hip-hop generally signifies the musical genre, and the term has spread around the world due to the proliferation of hip-hop albums and singles. Some of the world's most popular and acclaimed music stars are hip-hop artists. When people express opinions on "the state of hip-hop" and "where hip-hop is going," they are usually referring to hip-hop as a musical genre.

Lord Jamar, Brand Nubian

Hip-hop is one of the most influential musics in the world. . . . There's so many different genres of hip-hop now. There's hip-hop that you hear on the radio, and there's the hip-hop that you don't get to hear, [where] the flows are dope and they're moving hip-hop forward in a different kind of way. And there's hip-hop that you get to hear all the time that's not doing that, that's dumbing it down, that's making it more simple, and they're not doing what I would like to see done.[5]

Buckshot, Black Moon

Hip-hop is surviving, longer than a lot of music has. It's surviving longer than disco, longer than [other genres]. Hip-hop has changed, but hip-hop is great, man, hip-hop to me is a beautiful, beautiful thing and in a beautiful place because . . . every time there's a new young generation there's a new form to give them, that's still hip-hop.[6]

The two main elements that make up hip-hop music are rapping and beatmaking. These are sometimes referred to as simply *beats and rhymes*, where *rhymes* refers to rapping, while *beats* are the instrumental tracks that are rapped over.

Artists and fans often use the term *beats and rhymes* when they're talking about the essence of the music. If a song is stripped back to just hard beats and rhymes, it could be considered more authentic than songs with elaborate choruses and melodies, which take the focus off the two central ingredients.

DJ Premier

His new album is strictly hard beats and rhymes.[7]

J-Ro, Tha Alkaholiks
The album basically, it's a lot of hard beats and rhymes . . . [8]

Inspectah Deck, Wu-Tang Clan
The classic Hip Hop beats and rhymes of the 90s and before . . . [9]

The term *beats and rhymes* is used often throughout the music, as in the title of A Tribe Called Quest's album *Beats, Rhymes, & Life*, and in the lyrics of many other notable artists' songs, such as Gang Starr's "Stay Tuned," De La Soul's "Verbal Clap," Queen Latifah's "Ladies First," LL Cool J's "Can't Think," and Dilated Peoples' "20/20."

Rapping

Rapping, also known as "MCing," refers to performing lyrics rhythmically to a beat as a type of vocal percussion, often with a heavy emphasis on rhyming and rhyme schemes.

Tech N9ne
Having the rhythm to being able to stay on beat, it made me sort of like a percussionist. I always wanted to play drums, so if you listen to my flow it's like I'm beating on bongos or something.[10]

Rah Digga
I like all the phrases, the whole line, to rhyme if I can help it. Instead of just the last two syllables in the line and two lines that rhyme, I like to rhyme four, five, six, seven syllables, like the whole line if I could, for as long as I can.[11]

This is done by a rapper or MC ("master of ceremonies")—these two terms are usually used interchangeably with no difference in meaning, although some artists make distinctions. "MC" is sometimes used to imply a greater degree of live performance skill.

Buckshot, Black Moon

A rapper is somebody who can rap on the mic and sound good and flow good and do it onto a beat and everything. An MC can grab that mic and control a party [like] Doug E. Fresh . . . he's a master of the ceremony, he's an MC.[12]

One Be Lo, Binary Star

Okay, I'm gonna be real picky about this. To me it's the difference between a rapper and an MC. Some people make amazing albums which makes them great, [where you say,] "He's a great recording artist, but he ain't a great MC, he can't rock the crowd." Most artists in general, I just think cats don't know how to rock the mic [at a live event]. Even people that's making amazing music, they still don't know how to perform. A lot of these cats, regardless of their level of talent and skill or whatever, they just don't know how to rock the crowds, so that's some MC shit to me. MCing is something totally different to me and only very few people can do that.[13]

Another use of the terms is to suggest that "rappers" are more commercially focused and less skillful, while "MCs" are more genuine, authentic, and proficient.

KRS-One

An MC is a representative of hip-hop culture. A rapper is representative of corporate interests. An MC can be a rapper, but a rapper will never be an MC. What we have today, are rappers.[14]

MC Lyte

When you're an MC, you completely know the difference, you know what's real. You know what's generated from the heart when you hear it. When I listen to [artists like] Nas, Jay-Z, those are MCs. But then you have rappers . . . they're kinda skating along, they're not risk takers.[15]

Contradicting this, however, is the use of the term *rapper* to describe artists who *are* credible and authentic, as described by equally knowledgeable hip-hop practitioners. This is usually because they are using *rapper* as a general term for someone who raps.

DJ Premier

[Jay-Z or Nas] . . . they rhyme differently. I think Nas is a iller lyricist on the mic, where Jay, it's not really an MC thing. Nas is an MC, Jay's a rapper, to me. But he's a good rapper though.[16]

Chuck D, Public Enemy

I must point out that if you had to look in a book for the definition of a rapper you would probably see a picture of Jay-Z.[17]

The definitions of the two terms regularly change from artist to artist, along with who is an MC and who isn't. Even though they are used interchangeably the vast majority of the time, there is still a lot of contention around the definitions of the terms and how they should be used.

Beatmaking

Beatmaking refers to hip-hop production—creating the musical backing that accompanies the rapping. This can be made in various ways: production equipment, "beatboxing" (where someone creates rhythmic drum sounds vocally), with a live band, or through a DJ manipulating records (see p. 111 for more on hip-hop instruments). There are some hip-hop releases that are actually *just* beats—this is generally referred to as "instrumental hip-hop," as heard on DJ Shadow's classic 1996 album, *Endtroducing.*

Tech N9ne
The beats tell me exactly what to do [when I'm rapping]. If the beats are not knocking, it won't motivate me to write anything. The beats tell me exactly what to do, the music moves me—the music makes me do it.[18]

Del the Funky Homosapien
The marriage between lyric and music is paramount. This is why artists can get away with saying nothing basically and still have a hot song—the first layer of musical pleasure is the sheer enjoyment of the sound of the music itself.[19]

Beats are made by a *beatmaker* or a *producer.* In other genres of music, a producer's job is generally to record a live band and make decisions about the overall sound of the record, often giving input into how the vocalist and musicians actually play the song. However, in hip-hop, the person who actually makes the musical backing is almost always credited as the producer, whether they provide this kind of input or not—the term *producer* in hip-hop is synonymous with the person who creates the music that will be rapped over. However, some hip-hop artists do make a distinction despite this widespread usage of the term *producer*.

Shock G, Digital Underground

I don't consider myself a producer, I'm just a musician who likes to mix and arrange stuff a bit. I never really "produced," per se, meaning I didn't shape or groom the other artists. I'd just take an idea as far as I could take it, and then leave the holes for the next rapper or musician to add their thing to it. I'm not the type to "shape" someone else's career . . . real producers help with all that stuff. If telling whoever is in the booth "yay or nay" as to whether they should redo a vocal or not, if that's considered producing, then everybody in Digital Underground was a "producer," because we all did that for each other. Whoever was at the board when you're in the booth was your producer, even the pizza guy. I wasn't 2Pac's producer, I was his piano player and keyboardist, his samplist, and so was Big D, who was also his DJ. Sure, maybe I stayed behind with the engineer to help mix the tracks that I laid, but does that make me a producer? Dr. Dre is a producer. Rick Rubin is a producer. Puffy is a producer for what he did with Biggie, because if you take Puffy out of the picture, a major hole is left in Biggie's program. But if you take any of 2Pac's beatmakers out of 2Pac's equation, you'd still have the same glorious—and tragic—career, just different music. Therefore, 2Pac was essentially his own producer, making his rounds and gathering his tracks and collaborators.[20]

There are occasions where the term *producer* is used to suggest someone is more skilled than being "just" a beatmaker, though these terms are not as heavily contested as *MC* and *rapper*.

Hip-Hop Culture

While this guide focuses on hip-hop as a genre of music, the musical elements are often said to be part of a broader hip-hop culture which contains additional "elements." As well as rapping and beatmaking (sometimes referred to as "DJing," because beatmaking evolved from DJing, see p. 9), it also includes the form of dance known as b-boying (commonly referred to as *breakdancing* by those outside the b-boying community) and also graffiti art.

Afrika Bambaataa, along with his Universal Zulu Nation, is widely acknowledged as having grouped these four elements together under the name "hip-hop."

Afrika Bambaataa
Hip-hop is different elements dealing with music, rap, graffiti art, b-boys, what you call break boys, or b-girls, what you call break girls.[21] The Zulu Nation has pushed [hip-hop] under the whole culture and we're the ones that brought it under the elements—the DJs, the MCs, the graffiti writers, the b-boys and b-girls—so we could make this whole cultural movement that's called hip-hop.[22]

This idea of the culture of hip-hop was then spread by the media, particularly in the early 1980s. As shown earlier, journalist and author Steven Hager is noted as one of the first journalists to write about hip-hop. Speaking with Afrika Bambaataa led to his use of the term *hip-hop* to describe the culture and the elements in one of the first published articles on hip-hop in 1982, as well as writing the book *Hip-Hop* in 1984. The grouping of these elements featured heavily in many early '80s movies and books, such as *Wild Style* and *Style Wars*.

Steven Hager

Bambaataa was smart enough to realize that they needed an overarching name to describe the culture—what it was. And so he used the name *hip-hop*. But the name *hip-hop* had never been used by anybody else.[23]

Jeff Chang

Hager made explicit what most other journalists had not, that the subcultures of b-boying, rap and graffiti were related. He wrote a book called *Hip Hop: The Illustrated History of Break Dancing, Rap Music and Graffiti*, tying together the [elements].[24]

The idea of hip-hop culture and its four elements of MCing, DJing, b-boying, and graffiti has been widely adopted by many people, including other notable hip-hop artists.

Grandmaster Caz

Graffiti is just as important in the culture of hip-hop. B-boying. What the media calls break-dancing . . . b-boying is not a multibillion-dollar industry because they don't know how to market it that way. But rap? MCing? Oh yeah, it just went through the roof. But it's only one element of the culture.[25]

R.A. The Rugged Man

There are different aspects to hip-hop: graffiti, DJing, the beat-making. For me, as a lyricist, I don't live all of that other stuff. I see other MCs sign their autographs and make their signatures look like graffiti. . . . I live my entire life for the lyricism in hip-hop. The culture is so much more broad than just what I do, but that's my entire life—lyricism and MCing.[26]

However, there are also people who have been heavily involved with the elements who don't subscribe to grouping these art forms all under the heading of hip-hop.

Prominent 1970s graffiti artists such as BLADE and FARGO suggest that the media spread the idea of the elements, even though it did not accurately represent reality. Pioneering hip-hop DJ and icon Grandmaster Flash has also questioned graffiti's inclusion as an element.

FARGO

I don't see the correlation. The correlation between hip-hop and graffiti, that's a media thing. And breakdancing—they put that all in one package, so they can identify it, put it in a box. There is no correlation between hip-hop and graffiti, one has nothing to do with the other.[27]

BLADE

They put hip-hop, breakdancing, and rap music and graffiti and all this stuff together, because it's something I guess they thought they could market [for] whatever the hell reason. But it has nothing to do with the original stuff, when [graffiti] writing came along in 1970. It's got nothing to do with anything . . . that's all '80s stuff.[28]

Grandmaster Flash

You know what bugs me, they put hip-hop with graffiti. How do they intertwine? Graffiti is one thing that is art, and music is another.[29]

An example of the packaging of the elements can be seen in the classic 1983 hip-hop movie *Wild Style*. The film had a big influence on people's perception of hip-hop and was one of the first places where all the elements were shown together. However, Charlie Ahearn, who directed the film, states that it did not represent reality.

Grandmaster Caz

I believe that *Wild Style* is the first time that all the elements of hip-hop were represented.[30]

Fab 5 Freddy

I had read somewhere [that] for a culture to be a complete form, it had to have art, music, and dance. That was the grain of what became *Wild Style*. I felt that seeing breakdancing, graffiti, rapping, and DJing in a film would only make the culture stronger.[31] I helped explain to people that graffiti was part of hip-hop. It was always something I saw as one cultural movement.[32]

Charlie Ahearn

In the summer of 1980, I was making an art show in an abandoned massage parlor in Times Square. Fab 5 Freddy started talking to me about making a movie about graffiti and rap music [which became *Wild Style*].[33] *Wild Style* is like a fantasy, it's not a documentary. Everything in *Wild Style* was made for the film, it was to project an image. And people saw that image and they carried it forward and built on that, but that wasn't really happening, that was just happening for the film.[34]

Ahearn suggests that the elements were a lot less integrated in reality than people may suggest in retrospect.

Charlie Ahearn

There were interconnections, but there were no visible signs of it. Like in the whole year that I was in the Bronx before the movie, I saw no b-boying—it simply wasn't there. It was going on somewhere else. B-boying was considered passé and out of fashion in the Bronx. People remembered it, but when I mentioned that it would be in the movie people would go, "Aww, that's been played out so long ago!" The MCs really were not into it. The b-boys were not really on the scene at the parties and events except Frosty Freeze. Likewise the people who were down with the graf scene weren't at those parties. The only one I saw was PHASE 2, because he did the flyers. Lee Quinones was a b-boy when he was a kid bombing trains [with graffiti], but he never went to the parties.[35]

Of particular contention is the specific inclusion of graffiti as an element of hip-hop. Graffiti icons such as LADY PINK (one of the stars of the film *Wild Style)* suggest that graffiti should be seen as an independent art in its own right and not just as an element of hip-hop.

LADY PINK

I don't think graffiti is hip-hop. Frankly I grew up with disco music. There's a long background of graffiti as an entity unto itself.[36]

It is noted by many of the prominent early graffiti writers such as COCO 144, PHASE 2, BLADE, and FUZZ ONE, as well as others throughout graffiti's history, that many graffiti writers did not and do not listen to hip-hop music. They also assert that modern graffiti's history pre-dates hip-hop—while hip-hop is widely considered to have been created in 1973 with Kool Herc's innovation in playing records (see p. 117), graffiti had been developing for a number of years prior to this.

STAY HIGH 149

I started [writing graffiti] in '69, man, there was another guy out there, his name was TAKI 183, another guy from the Washington Heights area [of New York]. He was a Greek kid and he started a little bit before I did.[37]

COCO 144

I was listening to jazz, Latin jazz, and rock. This was before hip-hop was created. Anybody that does their homework would know graffiti came first.[38]

PHASE 2

Fact . . . there is no way in the world that aerosol [graffiti] culture was spawned from hip-hop . . . it was going on years before that.[39] Aerosol culture was there before anyone even conceived of a thing called hip-hop.[40] Many [graffiti] writers never listened to rap, many writers were more partial to headbanging than head-spinning and a huge amount of rappers, breakers [dancers], and so-called "hip-hoppers" couldn't tell you the first thing about [graffiti] writing.[41]

FUZZ ONE

Graffiti came first, before everything else. . . . Before 1978, the graffiti soundtrack was more Led Zeppelin, Rolling Stones, Jethro Tull, Ted Nugent, Black Sabbath, [Bachman Turner Overdrive], the Eagles, and Lynryd Skynyrd.[42]

BLADE

When I was writing [graffiti], there was no hip-hop, there was no . . . there was none of that stuff. When we came along, we were listening to Sly & the Family Stone.[43]

LADY PINK

Many of the white people who write graffiti listen to rock'n'roll and don't know anything about hip-hop.[44]

A number of graffiti writers and scholars suggest that while graffiti and hip-hop have interacted with each other at various points, this does not necessarily mean that graffiti is an element of hip-hop.

Buddy Esquire

The only connection I could see is rap and graffiti are both from the ghetto, a lot of the original writers from back in the days came from the ghetto, so maybe that is why they can identify it as such. But also since every writer is not from the ghetto, not every writer is going to associate themselves with [hip-hop].[45]

Joe Austin

The lack of a common hip-hop formation before the early to mid-1980s means that [graffiti] writing has more than a decade of history before rap broke onto the popular music scene, and their later development, while connected, is by no means determining.[46]

B-boying has also distanced itself from hip-hop as a genre of music. B-boys often prefer to dance to other genres, such as the records that the original hip-hop DJs played and sampled from, rather than to music made by hip-hop artists.

Joseph Schloss

Due to the nature of the movements, the music cannot be significantly sped up or slowed down without altering the form of the dance. In fact, when the tempo of hip-hop music began to slow down in order to better emphasize the words of its MCs, b-boys collectively decided that, rather than change the dance to fit the new tempos, they would actually *reject* hip-hop music. To this day, dancers rarely break to contemporary hip-hop . . . [this] has reinforced the dance's estrangement from rap music.[47]

Phantom, Ready to Rock, Mighty Zulu Kings

I was introduced, basically, to James Brown, Jimmy Castor Bunch, and the rest of my life listened to that music and enjoyed that music and did the dance that went along with it . . . that's the original essence of the dance. It was inspired by that music. . . . You gotta keep doing it. . . . We were passed down those records, and now it's our time to pass those records down.[48]

Hip-Hop Vs. Rap

Another area of contention, similar to *rapper* vs. *MC*, is the use of the terms *hip-hop* and *rap*. When someone makes a distinction, they sometimes use *hip-hop* to refer to the culture and *rap* to refer to the music, or to just rapping, as an element of the culture. In this context, "rap" doesn't have a negative connotation, it's simply being used to describe one part of a bigger whole.

Grandmaster Caz

Rap is one thing; *hip-hop* is something else. Hip-hop is the entire culture, and rap is just one element of it.[49]

Afrika Bambaataa

Rap is part of hip-hop, hip-hop is not part of rap. People have to understand that. We put the term on it, the music "hip-hop," but now when you say "hip-hop," people just think, "Oh, you're talking about a rap record." And they're forgetting about the b-boys, the b-girls, graffiti artists, the MCs, and also the knowledge part of hip-hop.[50]

A variation of this is where *hip-hop* refers to the culture *and* the music, as long as it's music that represents the culture properly, while *rap music* is used to refer to more commercialized music. In this context, *rap* takes on a more negative meaning— music that is simply made for profit with no grounding in the culture.

K-Os

What I hear on the radio . . . I think it's *rap*. I don't think guys are hanging out with b-boys, checking graffiti, and listening to DJs . . . you're not really a part of a *hip-hop* ecosystem, per se. And that's a big difference . . . someone like Mos Def, he made some line about "I used to want to be a b-boy." All that kind of knowledge changes making songs . . . I think there's a love there, you know.[51]

However, most hip-hop practitioners use the two terms interchangeably to simply refer to the music, and often use the term *rap* even when talking about very critically acclaimed artists such as Rakim and Run-D.M.C., in direct contrast to the notion that *rap* describes more commercial music. In this context, *hip-hop* and *rap* both just mean the genre of music, with no negative connotations for either.

Big Noyd

I grew up around rap music all my life, listening to Rakim, Big Daddy Kane, Kool G Rap . . . and I used to write down a lot of their rhymes.[52]

Kool G Rap
I had to be about nine, ten years old when I first started hearing hip-hop music being played out in the parks.[53]

2Mex
I learned from listening to other rap records like Slick Rick and Run-D.M.C., Doug E. Fresh and Dana Dane, KRS-One . . . I would just memorize every rap song that I liked.[54]

Akir
I'm a child of 1979, so by the time I even understood what words were, there was hip-hop music being played somewhere.[55]

Lord Jamar, Brand Nubian
Every rap song that I thought was hot back in the day, [I memorized]! "Super Rhymes" by Jimmy Spicer, of course "Rapper's Delight," some songs by Spoonie G, "Love Rap," joints back in the day.[56]

In fact, artists will often use the two terms within the same sentence to refer to the genre of music.

Tech N9ne
There's something out there for you in the rap world, I love the state of hip-hop.[57]

Planet Asia
Run-D.M.C. is the greatest rap group of all time, I don't care what nobody says, they put the stamp on what hip-hop was.[58]

Some hip-hop artists object to the co-opting of *hip-hop* as a catch-all term, as it is often applied to things that have little or no relation to the music.

Questlove, the Roots

These days, nearly anything fashioned or put forth by black people gets referred to as "hip-hop," even when the description is a poor or pointless fit. "Hip-hop fashion" makes a little sense, but even that is confusing: Does it refer to fashions popularized by hip-hop musicians . . . or to fashions that participate in the same vague cool that defines hip-hop music? Others make a whole lot of nonsense: "Hip-hop food"? "Hip-hop politics"? "Hip-hop intellectual"? And there's even "hip-hop architecture." What the hell is that? This doesn't happen with other genres. There's no folk-music food or New Wave fashion, once you get past food for thought and skinny ties. There's no junkanoo architecture.[59]

2. Hip-Hop Music Appreciation

Some of the most common criticisms of hip-hop music come from a lack of understanding of hip-hop's own value system for evaluating good from bad.

DJ Premier

It's just like a language, you have to know *how* to listen to it. If you don't listen to it the right way, all it sounds like is just a whole bunch of noise with a lot of loud-ass beats bang, bang, banging. And if you don't know how to listen to it, it *doesn't* make sense. My mother's eighty, she doesn't know how to listen to no hip-hop.[1]

Many of the things hip-hop fans and aficionados look for in a hip-hop song are almost the *opposite* of what fans look for in other genres such as rock, jazz, and blues. For example, rappers often note the vast differences between writing a song to be sung and writing a rapped, hip-hop song.

Evidence, Dilated Peoples

People who sing . . . they can hold one note for so long and have to say so few words to get the message across. "I love you," "You're in my heart," "You'll be here forever," and "It's hard to sleep without you" . . . that's a whole verse right there if you held the notes right. With a rapper, we can't do that—that's not even half a bar.[2]

Understanding hip-hop's aims and how they differ from other genres is key to understanding the appeal of the music and properly evaluating it. It can be looked at in the same way as film criticism—a horror movie can't be judged by the same criteria as a children's movie, as it would be heavily criticized for being too graphic and not lighthearted enough. To fully appreciate hip-hop, you have to know what to listen for, rather than judging the music on a different set of values.

Rhythm and Rhyme Are More Important Than Melody

A frequent criticism of hip-hop, especially in the earlier days when it first emerged, is that it doesn't use much melody and that rappers aren't able to sing.

There are rappers who actually do use a lot of melody, such as Slick Rick, Snoop Dogg, and groups like Bone Thugs-n-Harmony and the Pharcyde who have half-sung deliveries and sections of songs with traditional singing. Also, producers such as Dr. Dre and DJ Quik use live musicians and incorporate a lot of harmony and melody in their music.

Big Daddy Kane
If you really, really want to look at it, [early hip-hop groups such as the] Cold Crush [Brothers], Fantastic, and Master

Don and the Def Committee, these cats when they performed were singing. When the Force MDs were the Force MCs they were like, "here is our rap group," but when they were doing their routines they were singing. The only time they were rapping is when they would freestyle one by one, but the majority of their routine was straight up singing. So that whole melodic thing has always played an important part in hip-hop from the beginning.[3]

Shock G, Digital Underground

[There] was the '80s wave of hybrid hip-hop groups and melodic MCs, like Jimmy Spicer, Planet Patrol, Full Force, Jonzun Crew, [Slick Rick, also known as] MC Ricky Dee's outrageous singing on "La di da di," and especially Queen Latifah, who took rap-singing to a whole 'nother level of believability and harmonic accuracy when she dropped the game-changing "Wrath of my Madness / Princess of the Posse" single in '88.[4]

However, these are exceptions, as most hip-hop music emphasizes the rhythms and rhymes of the rapping, coupled with the rhythms of the "beats" (as the musical backings are usually referred to).

Rhythm

Hip-hop music normally revolves around the rapping and the musical backing and how these two elements interact. The musical backing is usually based on repetition, with the same or similar rhythms repeated constantly throughout a track. The rapping creates variation and continually changes—it is common for the rapped rhythms to change in every line of a verse.

These two elements complement each other by doing opposite things. It's easier to appreciate the changing rhythms of the rapping when you have the stable, repeating rhythm of the musical backing to compare it to. If they both varied, there wouldn't be this contrast, and if they both stayed the same, there wouldn't be any variation to create interest and surprise. Because of this, experimenting and playing with different rhythms is a big part of the artistry of the rapper.

Aesop Rock

A lot of those little patterns and rhythms are what people find attractive about [hip-hop music and rapping]—it's such a rhythmic form of vocals.[5]

Del the Funky Homosapien

Rhythmically, how you swing, and playing something funky or with a groove, is [like] you're playing with it. It would bore you to just sit up there and [rap] it normally, just straight and stiff, so to entertain your own self, you like doing other shit with it. Think of it like [this]: Somebody that's a pro at [the video game] *Street Fighter* is not gonna want to sit on *Street Fighter* and just play stiff, normally—they're gonna want to entertain themselves by doing [lots of techniques]! They're gonna floss with it a little bit. So anybody that's looking at them playing, it's damn near like watching a cartoon, they're so good.[6]

There are of course occasional exceptions to this—some songs do have musical backings which have significant changes throughout (such as work by DJ Shadow or J Dilla) and sometimes a rapper will decide to do a track using the same rapped rhythm all the way through (Gift of Gab of Blackalicious and Busta Rhymes have both used this kind of structure). But these are deviations from the standard template.

For many rappers the creative process begins with improvising rhythms before the lyrics are even written—the combination of the rhythm and rhymes of a rap are often referred to as the *flow*.

Royce Da 5'9"

I come up with the flow before I write anything down. Once I figure out the flow, then I gotta figure out the words and I just have to figure out how to fit the words into that flow. I usually pick the flow before I even start writing the verse.[7]

Masta Ace

What I do, I'll play the beat and I'll start mumbling words, a flow to that beat. And the words don't make any sense, they just sound like gibberish, but what I'm trying to formulate is how the [lyrics] that I'm gonna create are gonna flow into that beat. So the beat comes on, and I just start kinda mumbling, and once I get the bounce of how I wanna rhyme, then I start to turn those mumbles into actual words.[8]

With rhythm in hip-hop music, it's important to listen for the variations that the rapper uses, as well as the fixed rhythms of the musical backing. There will usually be drums doing one rhythm, bass doing a rhythm on top of that, and so on, stacked on top of each other to create the fixed musical backing that repeats. The rapper's varying rhythms sit on top of the rhythms of the musical backing, as another musical instrument.

Gift of Gab, Blackalicious

I'm basically trying to be like another instrument on the track. I want to ride it like the bass line is riding it, only with words. I wanna ride it just like the guitar or the violin or whatever instrument, just riding it.[9]

Rhyme

The other important element that listeners of other genres may not be used to assessing is rhyme. While you may get a few rhyming words at the end of each line of a regular rock song, for example, in hip-hop the most advanced rappers like to fill each line with a lot of rhyming words, often creating complex rhyme schemes that constantly change and evolve over a verse or song. A lot of rappers judge their peers on the work they put into their rhymes and rhyme schemes.

Eminem

You really gotta live it—my mind 24/7, aside from family stuff obviously, is constantly thinking of ways to bend words. What I love about rap, is it feels like puzzles to me, words are like puzzles and trying to figure out a puzzle, trying to figure out where it could go here, and how many words can I make [rhyme]. I'm real into the craft of just MCing and I always think like, "how can I figure this puzzle out?" Like how can I take words and put them at the end of the sentence, but in between maybe make some words rhyme that rhyme in between, like sandwich them. So sandwich those words and try to make them rhyme inside of the phrase and then come back outside and try to rhyme with the word that I ended on the snare [drum]. I'm kind of real into the technical part of it.[10]

Masta Ace

You got guys that just rhyme *cat* with *bat* and *hat*, and that's it, but there's so much more to it if you want to put some time in. To hear a whole album of *cat, bat, hat*, it just sounds boring. That's why as an artist, when I listen to other rappers, there's guys that I really appreciate because they'll come up with combinations of words that rhyme [where] I would have never thought of that.[11]

A heavy emphasis on rhyming is a key feature of the rapping styles of Kool G Rap, Big Pun, Eminem, and R.A. The Rugged Man, all known and lauded for their complex rhyme styles. Because other genres don't put as much emphasis on the level of rhyming in the lyrics, this is often overlooked by listeners who aren't used to this being a major feature of the music.

So where a listener expects to hear a melody, there often isn't one—instead the emphasis of the artist is on complex rhythms and rhyme schemes. These are the elements to listen for in order to get the most out of the technical side of rapping, as it is rare that melody will be the most prominent feature.

Playing with Language, Not Emotions

Another popular criticism of hip-hop music is that it doesn't engage listeners' emotions as often as other forms of music.

A number of hip-hop artists do specialize in emotional content—numerous classic hip-hop songs are notable particularly because of their emotional content, such as Pete Rock & CL Smooth's "They Reminisce Over You (T.R.O.Y.)."

Dante Ross

[Pete Rock & CL Smooth's song, "They Reminisce Over You (T.R.O.Y.)" is] a strange rap record to be a hit song, because when you're dealing with loops and rap music in general, especially at that time period, the music wasn't necessarily emotional. That song is like almost a blues song, it's very melancholy, and atypical of a hit rap record. It's a song that never goes away . . . it tells a story, CL is talking about how he met Trouble T Roy [who died accidentally] . . . "They Reminisce Over You" spells "Troy."[12]

Big Daddy Kane

When you look at artists like Melle Mel, Chuck D, 2Pac Shakur, when you look at artists like these cats, it's the type of thing where what they're talking about is something that you've experienced, something that you're probably having a problem with. And they just touched upon it in song and you felt it, because this is something that's been messing with you mentally. You felt it and it touched you that way—it hits your heart.[13]

However, many of the most acclaimed rappers aim to impress the listener with clever wordplay and flow, rather than trying to get a "deeper" emotional response. It can be equated with hearing an impressive solo on a percussion instrument, where the focus is on showcasing the technical proficiency of the musician. In hip-hop, this is sometimes done with the inventiveness of the content and other times it's done with impressive rhyme schemes and rhythms. It can also be done with rapid-fire, fast rapping styles, or styles that continually vary throughout a song.

Myka 9, Freestyle Fellowship

The average dope MC that's really tight, they'll tell you [that] in your mind you're constantly thinking of metaphors. Every time you see a street sign or a billboard, you're thinking, how can I tie that into a rhyme? So [you] constantly think of metaphors, analogies, things of that nature.[14]

If there does not seem to be an obvious attempt to connect with the listener in a deep, emotional way in a particular song, it's usually because the focus is on other areas. There may be a lot of rhyming words being used, the rapper might be employing a series of complex rhythms, or there could be a lot of wordplay or witty metaphors. Whereas a rock ballad would almost always try to give the listener an emotional response of some kind, this is often not the case with a lot of hip-hop songs, especially where it is a pure demonstration of skill.

It Can Be Flow and Delivery, Not Meaning

Hip-hop content can often confuse first-time listeners who are expecting the lyrics to have a clear meaning. For example, Das EFX's "They Want EFX" begins with lyrics which are essentially a collection of nonsensical sounds.

A lot of hip-hop lyrics do have an obvious meaning, especially if they are story raps, or raps filled with interesting metaphors and similes. In certain songs, hip-hop lyrics sound like they don't make sense until you understand the slang, such as a lot of Wu-Tang Clan or E-40 songs, which use very dense slang.

E-40

I was the first one who put [the slang term *fo' shizzle* meaning *for sure*] out there real tough in 1996 on my song "Rappers Ball." We were saying "fo' sheezy," and "fo' shizzle." I told Jay-Z after he used it on his record, I said, "That's a Bay Area word, man." That's from the land where they pop their collars and jack their slacks. Then I took it to "fo' shiggedy" to "fo' shiggadough" and now "fo' shiggadale," that's the newest. You know, it don't stop. 75 percent of the words I made up. Even before this rap game, my ear's always been to the street. I've been making up slang words since the first grade, you smell me? I stay coming with something to keep the game interesting. I tell them the rap game without [E-]40 is like old folks without bingo.[15]

But often the actual meaning of the words is secondary to the way the rap is being said, and to the rhythm and rhyme schemes—the flow of the rap. A string of rhyming words doesn't always have to "mean" anything in particular, it can just be an impressive run of words, like a drummer doing a fast drum roll. This explains the Das EFX example—it is an opening vocal drum roll of sounds, launching into the first verse.

Myka 9, Freestyle Fellowship

It's kinda gibberish if you're just writing and putting stuff down that you don't really understand, but even in that sense, gibberish is a style. There's many different styles to the form—we call that wild style, where you're just putting random words together because you like the way the syllables and the consonants ring.[16]

Often the actual topic is just a theme to riff on while coming up with creative flows and vocal styles. But when a run of rhyming words *does* make sense, it is always particularly impressive.

Tech N9ne

It's hard to rhyme and make sense at the same time . . . if I'm talking about something like [in the lyrics of "This Ring"]: "This ring, got me a top-notch, straight hot fox, we sought rocks . . . dropped two, playing hopscotch on the block," it sounds like just a lot of rhyming words, people love it, but if you listen to it, I'm talking about how I met my wife. "Got me a top-notch, straight hot fox, we sought rocks," [means] we went out and bought rings, "dropped two, playing hopscotch on the block" [means] we had two little girls. To make sense and still make it fun for the MC or the people to listen to, it's a hard thing to do.[17]

There isn't always a hidden meaning to untangle from every line of lyrics in hip-hop—sometimes the lyrics are meant to impress through how they sound, rather than through what they mean.

It Covers Its Own Subjects

Hip-hop's frequent focus on guns, sex, drugs, money, and bragging is easily one of the most common criticisms of hip-hop.

This complaint can come from too shallow a knowledge of hip-hop, as artists such as A Tribe Called Quest, the Pharcyde, Brand Nubian, X Clan, Public Enemy, Common, Mos Def, Blackalicious, and many more, have numerous songs with messages, positivity, and "substance" to their lyrics. Many of the more "positive" rappers strongly criticize the less positive rappers in the genre.

Melle Mel

I think if [certain rappers] would ever find something to say, [then they] would be decent at least. . . . Right now [some rappers just rap] about selling dope. [If] you're sitting on a half billion dollars—you can evolve them rhymes. You can say something that makes people see a whole different reality. [If a rapper is] a half billion up and the only thing he can talk about is how he used to sell [drugs]? You're proud of that? That's one of your high points? That should not be a high point in your life. That's not something you even let somebody else know, much less let them hear you say it with reverence and pride. Say it and then say, "But I'm doing a lot better now." Say what it really is. The difference between being good and great is when you can change other people's perceptions and realities. If people still think the same thing about you now, that they thought when you first came out, then you're doing the same thing. If you look at somebody who is considered great, they've changed people's perceptions. [Some rappers are] stuck in between talking about dope and killing people. I consider guys like that limited.[18]

Brother J, X Clan

We have the opportunity to take what we've learned from our teachers and our ancestors and put it into a major media forum. Hip-hop music is a powerful, powerful beast. It relates worldwide—everything is hip-hop. So for us to have the honor to do that here and the honor to put the message of freedom out, that's where our vibe comes from.[19]

However, a lot of hip-hop's classic records are based on more "negative" topics, such as acclaimed "gangsta rap" albums by N.W.A., Dr. Dre, Snoop Dogg, Notorious B.I.G., and 2Pac. Inventive lyricists, like in the group Clipse for example, use the topic of selling drugs to come up with creative ways to twist the English language again and again. Wu-Tang Clan's *36 Chambers* album includes many references to violence, yet it is a universally respected hip-hop masterpiece among hip-hop fans and critics.

Sean Price, Heltah Skeltah

[With] my subject matter, I'm not trying to save the world . . . it might be some crazy shit, but I know I'm writing the crazy shit, and I want to write the best crazy shit I can write.[20]

Again, it can be useful to compare hip-hop songs to films: there are good action films and bad action films, good horror films and bad horror films, good gangster films and bad gangster films. It is pointless to judge an action film using the same criteria you would use to judge a wildlife documentary and vice versa. *The Godfather* is one of the most acclaimed films of all time—though it's filled with violence. Similarly, rather than judging a hip-hop track on the topics it deals with, it's best to judge it on *how well* it covers those topics.

Crooked I

I don't care what you are—a political rapper, a conscious rapper, a gangsta rapper, a backpack rapper—[you have to] have some pride in the lyrics you're putting together, because it's important.[21]

Hip-hop often deals with life in inner cities and describes situations where violence and drugs are commonplace, as well as using extravagant imagery and metaphors. Braggadocio content and creating new ways of saying you're the best are integral to hip-hop and its history. Criticizing hip-hop for covering these topics is like criticizing the blues for focusing on "having the blues," or heavy metal for being too loud, or classical music for not having a strong enough drum beat.

Sampling & Sound Collage

Hip-hop's technique of sampling segments of other records is often misinterpreted as simply "stealing" other people's music or done because the artist didn't want to learn to play an instrument (many hip-hop artists do play instruments, but still sample records, as discussed on p. 122). However, it is almost always done for aesthetic reasons—sampling records creates a certain sound and feel that can't be acquired in any other way.

Kembrew McLeod

Whether one could exactly re-create a guitar riff [with session musicians] is a moot point for many hip-hop producers, because they want to access the sonic qualities that can only be found on a particular old album recorded in a specific time and place. They are looking for that certain kind of timbre, a certain kind of aura, that signifies, for instance, an old guitar sound taken from a funk-rock record from the 1970s.[22] [There are] certain sounds that can only be accessed through appropriation . . . the sonic qualities of vintage, analog equipment or a crackly vinyl record can't truly be recreated through digital plug-ins and audio filters. You can invoke these textures, but you don't get the same sound from a rerecording of a sample as you do from accessing that particular sound source.[23]

Although sampling has been the primary method for beatmaking overall, not all hip-hop records are created from samples. Hip-hop group the Roots play live instruments, producers such as Mantronix and the Neptunes often prefer to use keyboards and drum machines to create their compositions, and Dr. Dre regularly employs session musicians to either create original compositions or to replay samples. However, this live playing or replaying is often still judged on how closely it resembles the feel of the original samples.

Pete Rock

With the Roots . . . Ahmir ["Questlove" Thompson] is like the ultimate soul drummer. He's ill 'cause he listens to all kinds of drumming, from rock to soul to jazz. He's a beat-head. He can drum and it'll sound like an SP or MPC [sampling/sequencing machine].[24]

Dr. Dre

I don't really dig working with samples, because you're so limited when you sample . . . most of my music has been played. Back when we started with the N.W.A. thing, it was a lot of drum loops, drum samples, and what have you. But if we were going to sample something, we would try to at least replay it, get musicians in and replay it. If it was something we couldn't replay, we would use the sample. I've tried to stay away from it as much as possible throughout my career from day one.[25]

The core concept of hip-hop sampling is that records are a resource used to make music, creating a collage from parts of songs. This includes deciding which records to sample, which parts of those records are chosen, and how you combine and manipulate those sounds to create something new, using various forms of technology. This is hard to get used to for certain listeners, because it's so ingrained in other genres that the composer is held in the highest esteem and the credit should go to the people who "wrote" the music, rather than to anyone who has come along later and manipulated that music.

DJ Shadow

The sampling aesthetic, and the way that I make music, is rooted in the hip-hop paradigm and the hip-hop way of thinking, which is: take what's around you, and subvert it into something that's 100 percent you, but also has a cultural connection in the way that it was done before. Andy Warhol's pop art doesn't look like another guy's pop art—but they're rooted in the same aesthetic.[26]

As a hip-hop beatmaker, you might take the drums from the beginning of a rock song, the organ from the middle of a jazz record, the horns from a soul record, the bass from a funk record, and create a brand-new track.

Hank Shocklee, the Bomb Squad

When you're talking about the kind of sampling that Public Enemy did, we had to comb through thousands of records to come up with maybe five good pieces. And as we started putting together those pieces, the sound got a lot more dense.[27]

Domino

You gotta just take pieces and make them into a whole new thing. You find drum pieces and you can make different styles of drums, just by like piecing them, and making them your own thing.[28]

This sort of collage is common in other artistic fields. In the art world, a piece such as French artist Marcel Duchamp's *L.H.O.O.Q.*, where he added a mustache and beard to Leonardo da Vinci's *Mona Lisa*, is a good example of taking a significant portion of someone else's work and making minor changes to create something new and surprising. In literature, Tom Stoppard's play *Rosencrantz and Guildenstern Are Dead* uses characters and portions of text from Shakespeare's *Hamlet* and puts them in a new context, in much the same way as sampling does in hip-hop.

Chuck D, Public Enemy

We thought sampling was just a way of arranging sounds, to blend sound. Just as visual artists take yellow and blue and come up with green, we wanted to be able to do that with sound.[29]

Taking a sample from another genre and making a hip-hop record usually changes it significantly just by placing it in a starkly different genre, even if the riff is the same. For example, if you compare Dr. Dre's "Nuthin' But a 'G' Thang" to the record it samples, Leon Haywood's "I Want'a Do Something Freaky to You," it is immediately apparent that a section of music has been sampled. But they are significantly different overall as records in tone and genre—the hip-hop track sounds like a laid-back, West Coast, gangsta-rap track, with some aggression due to the lyrics. The song it samples from sounds like a funk/soul record with various musical movements throughout and it is essentially a love song. By putting the sample in a different setting, the same segment of music becomes something different and new—it is transformed.

Various "rules" often come into play when discussing the merits of a particular hip-hop song or producer, and these can vary from person to person. Credit is often, but not always, given to those who find rare records to sample, and who look to unusual genres for sampling material.

DJ Shadow

I sampled a lot of funk stuff that I was into at the time. I sampled a really long South Korean break-beat record that I've never found another copy of. The sample on [my track] "Building Steam" is from a kind of singer-songwriter thing—a lot of stuff that I was sampling was outside of the soul LP vein. Because still, a lot of people were only sampling stuff like P-Funk and Sly Stone, and, you know, more obscure records by groups like the Nite-Liters, or early Kool and the Gang stuff that's hard to find. But I was trying to find a sound different from everybody else's, so the source material had to be different from everybody else's. I was looking for records that I felt like were really obscure. Whether those were funk 45s, which nobody was up on yet, or kind of weird rock albums.[30]

Credit is also often given to beatmakers who use samples in particularly innovative ways. For example, chopping up a horn solo into twelve parts, rearranging those parts, and laying them over drums from somewhere else might be seen as more creative than simply repeating the main riff from a popular song.

Hank Shocklee, the Bomb Squad

Sampling was a very intricate thing for us. We didn't just pick up a record and sample that record because it was funky. It was a collage. We were creating a collage.[31]

Beatmakers with a purist approach, who continue to make hip-hop tracks the way they have traditionally been made, typically suggest that all sampling should be directly from vinyl records (rather than CDs or digital files) and should not include too much live instrumentation.

Jake One

There'll always be some sampled element in what I do. I think that's what kinda makes it hip-hop. If you're just playing . . . a bunch of instruments and there's no sampled drums, scratches or something, I don't think it's . . . I mean, it's hip-hop, I guess . . . I don't know. It just doesn't sound authentic. There's something about the way the old records sound when put together right. You can't really recapture 'em when you play [live].[32]

However, the final product is often the key measure—if it sounds great and works well with the rapping, even a simple looped sample can be held in high regard. Basic samples have formed the basis for a lot of hip-hop classics, such as Wu-Tang Clan's "C.R.E.A.M." and Cypress Hill's "Hits from the Bong."

Steinski

That's a stylistic thing [when someone samples a large piece of a record]. You can choose to be disappointed [that they didn't change it much, but] there's a lot of things I've heard where somebody picked up a chunk of something and used it—and it's like, man, that's really great! I'm not that discriminating [when it comes to how much is sampled and how much is changed]. I'm like Alfred E. Neuman [from the *Mad* magazine comics], walking around with this big smile on my face going, "Huh, huh, I like it," and that's pretty much it.[33]

Cut Chemist, Jurassic 5

I'll sample anything. My whole vinyl-only kind of banner-waving ways are dead. I think you have to embrace technology in order to grow as an artist and evolve. When I saw the CDJ I was sold. I was like, "cool, vinyl's done," and I was scratching on CDJ's. Not solely, but I'm down to use it. And [digital DJing system] Serato. But you know, I sample off vinyl, I sample off a lot of cassettes, a lot of stuff I use are live recordings that maybe nobody else used. So I'll use that and also sample live musicians.[34]

3. Debunking Hip-Hop Myths

Many hip-hop myths originate from within the hip-hop community itself. A lot of these myths are well intentioned—they are meant to help boost hip-hop's stature by highlighting a positive aspect or by providing a counterargument to a common criticism. For example, people sometimes attempt to tie political motivations to hip-hop's inception to illustrate its worthiness, importance, and depth, and it is commonly argued that practitioners *had* to use samples because they couldn't afford instruments, in response to the criticism that they were "stealing" other people's music.

However, hip-hop does not need to rely on these myths and fallacies to validate itself. While often well meaning, they usually obscure a more important, fundamental point, as we'll see.

Myth: People Sampled Records Because They Were Too Poor to Afford Instruments and Lessons
Fact: Beatmaking Equipment and Record Collections Are Expensive, and Traditional Instruments Were Not "Cool"

This is one of the most widely held assumptions about hip-hop music, even though it's one of the most implausible. While it is true that hip-hop came from harsh socioeconomic conditions, its practitioners were not usually so poor that they were unable to afford instruments. Many musicians are able to teach themselves inexpensively, with a secondhand acoustic guitar and a book of chords, for example, and there is always the option to sing.

During hip-hop's infancy, DJs would battle each other with sound systems—specially built with multiple speakers and amplifiers designed to be louder than other systems. Building one of these systems was not cheap as it meant collecting numerous pieces of hardware. The sound systems would often be expensive enough that DJs would enlist a gang to protect the system.

Kool DJ AJ

DJs used to battle: you would bring your sound system, I would bring my sound system. . . . You had to bring your gang for protection, because my system might have cost like $15,000, which I paid out of my own pocket, and if you didn't have no gang behind you, you might've lost your system in the South Bronx.[1]

Prince Paul

DJ stuff was more expensive back then than it is now. I mean, like way more expensive. So for them to even say that [people couldn't afford instruments] is crazy.[2]

DJ Kool Akiem

I mean DJing, if you're serious, you're gonna have to spend a thousand dollars on your equipment . . . then every record's ten bucks. Then you got speakers and blah, blah, blah. Even saying that [people were too poor to afford instruments] is kinda weird. Obviously, [the academics] just probably didn't think about it. The most important thing to them is, "Oh, the kids are poor," you know what I mean? Not even thinking about it. Just like, "Well, that must be it: they're poor!"[3]

Once hip-hop reached its golden age (as discussed on p. 147), one of the most frequently used pieces of production hardware for making hip-hop beats was the E-mu SP-12 released in 1986, along with its even more popular successor, the E-mu SP-1200, released in 1987 (see p. 123). A large number of classic hip-hop albums were made using one of these machines, and although they may seem primitive by today's standards, at the time they were cutting-edge, powerful, and expensive pieces of equipment.

Large Professor
This is the early days and an SP-1200 was a $2,500 machine. Anybody didn't just have an SP-1200.[4]

DJ Kool Akiem
Those samplers were [expensive] back then! I mean, you gotta have money, some way, to put your studio together. . . . Producing takes more money than playing an instrument. You play an instrument, you buy the instrument and then you go to class.[5]

Part of the myth also suggests that hip-hop artists weren't able to afford or get access to lessons or classes to learn traditional instruments. Again, this is denied by many notable hip-hop artists— often stating that the real reason they didn't learn traditional instruments is because it wouldn't have been seen as "cool" and they couldn't get the same aesthetic of sampled records just by learning a regular instrument.

Prince Paul

You know, everybody went to a school that had a band.
You could take an instrument if you wanted to. Courtesy
of your public school system, if you wanted to. But man,
you playing the clarinet isn't gonna be like, BAM! KAH!
Ba-BOOM-BOOM KAH! [like the drums from sampled
records]. . . . It wasn't that "Yes, yes y'all—y'all—y'all—
y'all," with echo chambers. You wasn't gonna get that [with
a clarinet].[6]

DJ Disco Wiz

[I could have been a member of the school band if I had
actually wanted to, it just wasn't cool] . . . I had enough
trouble just walking down the street without a fucking
trombone in my hand.[7]

The late Jam Master Jay of Run-D.M.C. also confirms that kids did
often play traditional instruments initially, but there was a certain
attraction to the turntables that drove many to become DJs.

Bill Adler

[Jam Master Jay, of Run-D.M.C.] first got involved with
music when he was about ten, learning drums and bass, and
playing in different bands.[8]

Jam Master Jay, Run-D.M.C.

All of a sudden, *the DJ* became the main attraction. He'd
come to a party with a turntable and giant speakers and records. Everyone stopped wanting to be in a band and started
spinning records instead . . . my moms got me a mixer, and
I started off like that.[9] I wanted to be a drummer, then I
saw Grandmaster Flash. That changed everything. When

hip-hop came to the neighborhood, it was like basketball—
you had to know how to do it.[10]

Many hip-hop artists originally learned instruments, but then left
them out of their hip-hop music, as they could not get the same
sound that sampling provides. Some, such as Shock G from Digital Underground, still play instruments and use them within
their hip-hop production.

DJ Jazzy Jay, Jazzy 5, Soulsonic Force
I was like, okay, I've got this fifteen-piece drum set up-
stairs that I took since I was eight years old, building up,
and now I've got to make room for some turntables.[11]

E-40
I was in the marching band from the fourth grade all the
way to the twelfth grade, see, and I played the drums, I
was in the percussion, in the drum line, so that's what my
thing was, so that's how I did it.[12]

Flavor Flav, Public Enemy
I play fourteen different instruments . . . I cut classes hanging out in the band room. . . . You're definitely gonna see
me out there as the drum major leading the band.[13]

Shock G, Digital Underground
I learned bass and drums first around age eleven, then sang
in a barely organized funk group called Parliament 2 at age
thirteen . . . we won our school's talent show that year
with a sick performance of "Flashlight" that sent the audience into a mild riot! At age fourteen, I took a hiatus from
funk music, traded my instruments for turntables, locked

myself in a room all summer practicing, and emerged as a competent hip-hop DJ.[14]

Too Short
I used to be a drummer in a band—elementary school, high school—and I took pride in being a good drummer.[15]

Learning instruments has also helped a lot of beatmakers and MCs with their hip-hop music.

DJ Premier
I took piano lessons, [but that's] something you don't get [immediately] when you were a kid. I was like, "Mom, I don't wanna do this. Boys don't do this." So I quit. But I found myself knowing where middle C is. When I was a kid I always knew where middle C was and e-g-b-d-f lines of the staff and f-a-c-e, the spaces, I always remembered that. Now that I do hip-hop, I'm back to it. I do a lot of hunting and pecking but I can do chords. I play piano, too. I'm not ill or anything, but I can do a little something. I play drums, I play bass, I play guitar. I played guitar in church. I played alto sax in school.[16]

Myth: Hip-hop's Musical Innovations Were Made Because of Harsh Social Conditions
Fact: Hip-hop's Musical Innovations Were Made Because They Sounded Good

There is a popular myth that suggests hip-hop music began as a way for the youth at the time to express their frustrations and to rail against authority figures—as a politically inspired art form birthed from harsh socioeconomic conditions. This is an overly romanticized view of hip-hop's creation that contradicts the facts.

While it's true that conditions were often very tough during hip-hop's inception, many hip-hop artists have pointed out that this was not one of the reasons for hip-hop music's creation.

Prince Paul

It wasn't cats sittin' around like, "Man. Times are hard, man . . . a can of beans up in the refrigerator. Man, I gotta—I gotta—I gotta—do some hip-hop! I gotta get me a turntable!" It wasn't like that, man. Ask Kool Herc! He was the first guy out there. I know him, too. We talked plenty of times. He's not gonna sit there and be like, "Man. It was just so hard for me, man. I just felt like I needed to just play beats back to back. I had to get a rhymer to get on there to make people feel good, 'cause times was just so hard." Yeah, cats kill me with that.[17]

DJ Kool Herc

I love my music, I love my sound system, and I just love to see people having fun. Period.[18]

Bill Adler

Russell [Simmons, cofounder of the pioneering hip-hop label, Def Jam,] went to the shows not just because he was in a gang and it was "something to do," but because he truly loved the music—particularly a certain beat in the music.[19]

Run, Run-D.M.C.

The worst thing that ever happened to me as a kid was that gym class would run out of time and I couldn't play my basketball game. Oh yeah, I couldn't bring my radio to school neither. But that's it. No way was I brainwashed or hurt by being black. It's not like I never had any money. I always had money.[20]

The most obvious area that early politicized expression would take place is in the content of rap lyrics, where issues could be presented clearly. And while highly political subject matter has been addressed through rapping in *later* hip-hop, the early, formative years saw the focus mainly on announcements, partying, and braggadocio.

Grandmaster Caz

At the time . . . the microphone was only used for announcements—to let people know where the next party was, maybe to shout somebody out in the crowd, or big me up while I'm on the turntable, [DJing], like, "Yeah, my man Casanova Fly is on the wheels of steel. Check him out, check him out."[21]

The early focus on party rhyming can be seen in the reaction to Grandmaster Flash and the Furious Five's 1982 song, "The Message," which is noted for being political *in contrast* to all the hip-hop music that had come before it, highlighting how rap did not start out as politically motivated, only gradually covering political content much later.

Kool Moe Dee

In 1982, Melle Mel caused another paradigm shift . . . Melle Mel shifted lyrical content with "The Message." Up until this point, there had only been party hits with light-hearted lyrical content. People didn't even know that hip-hop could have another voice that was outside of a party.[22]

Outside of the content of hip-hop songs, there is even less of a link between the early musical innovations and any form of politically motivated expression. For example, one of the key innovations that created hip-hop music was where DJs would take the most rhythmically energetic part of a record called the "break," or "breakbeat," usually where the music broke down to just drums and percussion for a while, and they would repeat just these parts back-to-back (see p. 133).

Afrika Bambaataa
The break beat is that part that you look for in a record that lets [you] just get wild. Then as soon as that break beat leaves, you say, "Aww, it's only a minute? It's only thirty seconds?" You know, you want to hear some more. So that's where the hip-hop DJs came in and started making that beat, that break beat, that stripped-down funk, expand longer and longer, so you could just get crazier and crazier and crazier on the dance floor.[23]

This was done because it sounded good to the people dancing and to the DJs. It wasn't a politically inspired technique, it was an aesthetic choice—take the parts of a record that you consider to be the best and repeat them. Another example can be seen when Grandwizard Theodore explains how he created a now standard hip-hop DJing technique, the turntable "scratch."

Grandwizard Theodore
I was always in my house trying to think of new ways to be different. One particular day I was in the house practicing, and the music was a little bit too loud, so my moms came and banged on the door . . . while she was talking to me, I was still holding the record. . . . When she left the room, I thought about what I was doing; [I was scratching the re-

cord back and forth on the turntable while holding it] and I was like, "Wow, this really sounds like something." I practiced with it and perfected it and used it with different records, and that's when it became a scratch.[24]

Theodore says he was always trying to "think of new ways to be different," and when he found a sound he liked, he incorporated it as a technique. He did not scratch a record back and forth because times were tough and he did not do it as a political statement—the technique came from an accident that sounded good, and further development of the technique came from a desire to innovate musically.

Similarly, Rakim's big impact and innovation with rapping (more on p. 80) was adding more complexity to the rhythms and the "flow" that rappers use. A political motivation did not drive him to update rap's flow—he did it because he was musically "shooting for something different" and he was mimicking a saxophone player with his way of rhyming.

Rakim

I was shooting for something different. Like, some of my influence was John Coltrane—I played the sax, as well. So listening to him play and the different rhythms that he had: I was trying to write my rhymes as if I was a saxophone player.[25]

Other notable developments and innovations discussed elsewhere in this book—Marley Marl's use of the sampler, Melle Mel's rapping in time to the beat, Kool G Rap's use of rhyming words, Grandmaster Flash's DJing techniques, Paul C.'s chopping of samples—tell the same story: hip-hop music was created from the love of musical innovation and from finding sounds and music that you liked, without any particular political focus or aims until later in its history.

Prince Paul

Loving the music in general. It's just the feeling that you get when you DJ. Especially back in the days. You can't even describe the whole feeling of how it was, because everything was so new and fresh. . . . It was all about fun. And it was a lot of fun. . . . [Hip-hop] was cool! It's like: we liked the music.[26]

Myth: Hip-Hop Requires You to Be "Real" and "Authentic"
Fact: A Lot of the Best Hip-Hop Uses Fiction

While there is a lot of hip-hop music that focuses on nonfiction and accurate accounts of life with little embellishment, hip-hop also has a long tradition of fictional creativity, incorporating wildly fantastical elements for entertainment and artistic reasons.

An impression you can get from a cursory listen to the music and the way some of the artists portray themselves, is that being authentic and "truthful" is paramount in hip-hop. But listening to a wide array of hip-hop records makes it clear that being "real" is rarely ever necessary, as long as the music is creative and entertaining.

Andy Cat, Ugly Duckling

A lot of rap is autobiographical—it's talking about where you're from, and your life, and all of that, but I got news for you, [many classic hip-hop artists,] they used to make it all up. They weren't going out killing people every night—it's called creativity.[27]

There are many examples of hip-hop songs based on fictional subject matter, such as sci-fi and fantasy—for example Rakim on Eric B. & Rakim's classic "Follow the Leader" and many of Kool Keith's lyrics. Just as every book is not a nonfictional account of actual events, hip-hop songs aren't either.

Lateef, Latyrx

I think it's kind of limiting to go, "Oh, it's gotta be real," because a lot of ideas are good that aren't real. Anything that I come into contact with [can influence the style]. Fictional stuff can easily be part of what I'm talking about—I could watch a sci-fi movie and write a song about it.[28]

A lot of the more battle-oriented hip-hop tracks, where a rapper may insult real or imaginary opponents, often use graphically vivid and fictional imagery for effect.

Vinnie Paz, Jedi Mind Tricks

When you're just doing some battle shit, and when you're saying you're going to chop someone's head off, it's not necessarily very realistic. So it's really whatever the song calls for.[29]

A lot of the braggadocio in earlier hip-hop was not based on reality, instead revelling in extravagant fantasies. As hip-hop has allowed some artists to actually attain the wealth and status that they talk about on records, listeners sometimes make the mistake of assuming hip-hop was always about being 100 percent authentic.

Kool G Rap

[When hip-hop began and] you talked that millionaire shit, you was just rapping. You didn't think no shit like that was possible. A mansion and a yacht? That was some cartoon shit. Now the shit is a reality and these kids today is just rapping for that.[30]

Myth: Rapping Came from the *Dozens*
Fact: Rapping Came from Announcements and Encouraging the Crowd to Party

When tracing the roots of rapping, literature on hip-hop often suggests that rapping came from the *dozens*. The dozens is a type of competitive insult game, such as "ya mama" jokes where competitors come up with creative jokes about each other's mothers, trying to outdo each other—it existed long before hip-hop. It's easy to see how the myth came about and how a connection was made, because a lot of later hip-hop includes graphic language and battling, which is also common within the dozens. Therefore, according to the myth, rapping must have come from the dozens as they share some similar features and because the dozens predates hip-hop.

However, you would then expect to find plenty of instances where hip-hop pioneers mention how they used to play the dozens, before later transferring it to the microphone at parties and clubs to create rapping, but this is not the case. Instead, the pioneers talk about how the microphone at parties and clubs was used to make announcements, call out friends, and to introduce the DJ.

Coke La Rock
Me and [Kool] Herc really got real tight, we started hanging together and rolling, then he said he was gonna have a party . . . [his sister] Cindy's birthday party [in 1973, which is often considered to be the "birth of hip-hop"]. [There was talking on the microphone at that party], but just calling out my friends' names, I was calling guys'

names out. I was saying like, my crew . . . and I would tell you, "go move your car." Like, "Easy Al, you're double parking me, go move your towns-car." And we're like fifteen, sixteen, so you'd be like, "All right, I'm gonna move my car!" So the girls would be like, "Ooh, he's got a car!" [But] you ain't got no car out there! So, that's all it was, it was hyping us up and laughing, dancing, talking.[31]

Keith Keith, Funky Four Plus One
[In hip-hop's early years] all the groups had MCs but the MC wasn't into rhyming or unity yet, they were just talking, like radio announcers. Then it got to a point where somebody started, "Hip, hop, hip hipity hop" and "To the beat y'all, freak freak y'all." And people started wanting to hear that.[32]

Kurtis Blow
Before 1976, MCs would just work the crowd; introduce people and stuff. "You're rocking with the number one DJ, somebody say, 'Oh yeah,'" type of stuff.[33]

The announcements developed into rhyming phrases and chants that were used to get the crowd excited and engaged.

Kevie Kev, Fantasic Freaks
The MCs was just more or less there to get the people involved, we would create the crowd participations: "All the hoes, say ho!" Anything that had to do with the crowd was where the MC, the master of the ceremonies, got involved.[34]

The short rhyming phrases then turned into longer sentences and eventually became regular on-the-beat rapping, in time with the music—Grandmaster Caz explains how it gradually evolved.

Grandmaster Caz

When I started out as a DJ [before I became a rapper], MCing as an art hadn't been formulated yet. The microphone was just used for making announcements, like when the next party was gonna be, or people's moms would come to the party looking for them, and you have to announce it on the mic, "So and so, your mother's looking for you at the door." You know, that kind of thing. So different DJs started embellishing what they were saying. Instead of just saying, "We'll be at the P.A.L. next week, October this and that," they'd say, "You know next week we gonna be at the P.A.L. where we rock well, and we want to see your face in the place," little things like that. . . . I would make an announcement this way, and somebody would hear me, and then they'd go to their party and they add a little twist to it. Then somebody would hear that and they add a little bit to it. I'd hear it again and take it a little step further 'til it turned from lines to sentences to paragraphs to verses to rhymes.[35]

Rather than using the preexisting put-downs of the dozens, rapping grew organically from the party scene. The early phrases were not competitive insults, but announcements, introductions, and call-and-response party chants.

The dozens appeared later, in certain songs, such as the Pharcyde's "Ya Mama" and in rap battles, where competitors do insult each other in a creative way, but these were ways of *using* rapping, rather than something that *created* rapping. To use an alternate example, there are rap songs about chemistry (Blackalicious's "Chemical Calisthenics"), but rapping didn't "come from" chemistry or "have its roots in" chemistry, as this particular myth suggests with the dozens.

Myth: A *Freestyle Rap* Was Originally an Improvised Rap
Fact: A *Freestyle Rap* Was Originally a Written Verse, on No Particular Subject

This is a myth that circulates heavily among hip-hop fans. The idea is that if a rapper says he or she is doing a freestyle rap, then this means it is a rap that has been improvised on-the-spot, like a jazz musician might improvise a solo. Rappers are sometimes chastised if fans think they pre-wrote the rap, using "writtens" (referring to pre-written lyrics), rather than improvising the lyrics.

While it is true that the term has widely come to refer to this kind of improvised performance, the term did not originally refer to improvised lyrics. This is a big point of contention, because hip-hop fans will often refer to "real," "original" freestyles or the "true" meaning of freestyling, without realizing that the original freestyles were not improvised—they were written verses which did not stay on any particular subject.

Big Daddy Kane

That term, *freestyle,* is like a new term, because in the '80s when we said we wrote a freestyle rap, that meant that it was a rhyme that you wrote that was free of style, meaning that it's not [on] a [particular] subject matter—it's not a story about a woman, it's not a story about poverty, it's basically a rhyme just bragging about yourself, so it's basically free of style. . . . That's really what a freestyle is. Off-the-top-of-the-head [rapping], we just called that "off the dome"—when you don't write it and [you] say whatever comes to mind.[36]

Divine Styler

In the school I come from, freestyling was a nonconceptual written rhyme . . . and now they call freestyling off the top of the head, so the era I come from, it's a lot different.[37]

Kool Moe Dee

There are two types of freestyle. There's an old-school freestyle that's basically rhymes that you've written that may not have anything to do with any subject or that goes all over the place. Then there's freestyle where you come off the top of the head . . . back in the day it was called, "coming off the top of the head." Before the '90s it was about how hard you could come with a written rhyme with no particular subject matter and no real purpose other than showing your lyrical prowess.[38]

Myka 9 of Freestyle Fellowship talks about how freestyle originally meant written rhymes, but was later redefined to refer to improvised rapping.

Myka 9, Freestyle Fellowship

Back in the day freestyle was bust[ing] a rhyme about any random thing, and it was a written rhyme or something memorized. We have redefined what freestyle is by saying that it's improvisational rap like a jazz solo, so as a result we actually helped create another trend and culture, another pastime.[39]

Although improvised rapping has become a complex art in its own right since the 1990s, this latter definition and style was not originally respected, as Kool Moe Dee explains.

Kool Moe Dee

A lot of the old school artists didn't even respect what's being called freestyle now . . . any MC coming off the top of the head wasn't really respected. The sentiment was MCs only did that if they couldn't write. The coming off the top of the head rhymer had a built-in excuse to not be critiqued as hard.[40]

Myth: Hip-Hop Doesn't Respect Other Genres of Music
Fact: Hip-Hop Artists Draw Influence from a Wide Variety of Other Genres

An assumption sometimes made about hip-hop artists is that they are musically ignorant—the argument assumes that because they don't adhere to the usual template of traditional instruments and melody, then they must be uninformed about other musical genres.

However, as hip-hop production is grounded in sampling from other music, many beatmakers have an extensive knowledge of other musical genres and obscure records. In fact, being familiar with a huge array of records in many different styles is often considered a key component to being a hip-hop DJ and beatmaker.

DJ Premier

I used to beg my mother to let me go see Parliament . . . I went to Chaka Khan with her . . . [she] took me to a Quincy Jones concert. I'm really big on concerts . . . I went to Iron Maiden, I went to Ozzy Osbourne, I've been to Van Halen, before David Lee Roth left the group . . . I went to Genesis, went to Phil Collins . . . I went to Mötley

Crüe . . . I went to U2, way back. I was into U2 from their first album. 1981, I think it was, when they came out with *Boy* and then *October.* I was a U2 fan from back then. And it was rebellious . . . I'm really into lyrics, and I used to hear what they sang; they were always protesting war and stuff. . . . I went to the Police before they broke up. I remember all this shit, and all that applies to what I do now![41] I was into punk rock, new wave—Duran Duran, Siouxsie and the Banshees, the Smiths. You know, groups that you'd be like, "Damn, Premier listens to that shit?" Hell yeah! Because it was good music . . . good music is good music![42]

Brother J, X Clan

I'm from the generation of those who dug in the crates, so much music has influenced me. . . . You can think about music like Isaac Hayes, excellent production, I can go to my mother's old college crates and look at Barbra Streisand and get a lesson about projection—there's so many different areas of music when you're just listening to love music, so my influences go heavy, man. Funk is a very heavy influence on me, I love the freedom of funk music, you look at George Clinton, you look at Sly Stone, you look at Sun-Ra . . . you look at the monsters of the science of funk, man, that's a whole different beast too. So I'm influenced by the ancestors and their creativity, man. All of it that came out on the wax and all of it that we have to interpret through time as we learn how to listen to music better. I'm a universal listener of music, so you can hear classical music when I'm in my car, or see me with a Walkman on with some heavy metal or I may be listening to some old-school music or some new-school instrumentals or whatever, however they divide it into these slots.[43]

MURS

When I'm writing an album, I tend to not listen to any rap at all . . . I usually take one country artist . . . one white music genre, one old soul music artist, and one jazz artist and I just go through all their work. Sometimes it's the Beatles, sometimes it's Johnny Cash, Curtis Mayfield, Miles Davis, John Coltrane . . . just to have as inspiration as I'm writing that record. I'm a fan of like Johnny Cash . . . Bernie Taupin and Elton John where they write songs where it's amazing—sometimes you don't even know what they're talking about but it still takes you somewhere. [And] I go to a lot of punk shows and hard-core shows and I've seen Tito Puente, Sergio Mendes. I go everywhere and just try to incorporate elements of other music into our performances.[44]

Grandmaster Caz

Hip-hop is not made up from scratch, the music and the foundation of the music of hip-hop comes from records that we found in our parents' crates. Old funk and soul grooves, we've given new life to artists like James Brown and Isaac Hayes and Sly and the Family Stone and George Clinton and Parliament and Funkadelic and so many other groups, because we're rapping over their beats.[45]

Some producers are even influenced by the behind-the-scenes methods used to construct a lot of older music, including how different songwriting teams would create records.

Pharoahe Monch

[P Diddy] is big on Motown and big on Berry Gordy, Tammi Terrell, Marvin Gaye—[they] would write songs for people, they had a team of writers and producers that would write songs for that artist . . . that is his music model.[46]

A lot of hip-hop artists are particularly knowledgeable about jazz, as it has been a source of inspiration and influence on both beat-making and rapping.

Lateef, Latyrx

I always recommend young MCs to listen to Lambert, Hendricks & Ross, they did a lot of jazz scatting stuff. They had a song called "Cloudburst" that's light years ahead of a lot of the stuff a lot of [hip-hop] MCs are doing now. That was in the '50s and that is as good or better than most cats are rapping right now, probably better.[47]

Pharoahe Monch

[Using your voice in rapping is like] with a sax or a horn up in the higher range of pitches, you can sound like a bird or you can sound frustrated, [and] in the lower ranges, you could sound aggravated or fat or jolly, like an elephant, and jazz musicians used this because most of their works are instrumentation. So if John Coltrane is doing a piece called "Africa," and he wants to convey to the listener how beautiful he thinks elephants are, it'd probably be in the lower range. And how fast he thinks a cheetah is or how beautiful a cheetah is, it'd probably be [in the mid-to higher ranges] and with very quick rhythms, painting a picture.[48]

Shock G, Digital Underground

My friend Saafir, a West Coast underground champion, once told me he gets his word patterns from jazz horn players like Charlie Parker and John Coltrane, [and] he swings his words around the beat rather than on it.[49]

Planet Asia

[My rap flow comes from] jazz music—it has a pattern but it doesn't have a pattern, it's free to go in any direction you want it to go.[50]

Reggae and ragga styles of music have also had a sizeable influence on hip-hop music.

Wise Intelligent, Poor Righteous Teachers

[Using the Jamaican style of rhyming and faster rhythms came from] a lot of reggae, a lot of reggae music in the community we grew up in, a lot of yard parties. There'd be dub sessions at everybody's house—a lot of Jamaican kids in the community, so we were at the dub sessions all the time, so it became a part of us.[51]

Myth: Rap Is Best Looked at as Poetry
Fact: Rap Is More Like a Form of Vocal Percussion

There are many well-intentioned people who compare rap to poetry—they are usually using traditional poetry as a high-water mark and trying to elevate the "worth" of hip-hop lyrics by making favorable comparisons. They are also often interested in analyzing hip-hop lyrics and want to use the same tools they use to analyze poetry.

Although you can read rap as if it were poetry, it unfortunately means that you miss much of the skill and finesse of rapping, which is found in the flow and the delivery. A lot of MCs state that it isn't even an equal balance—they suggest that the flow and delivery are actually the *main* elements of rapping, with content and poetic value as secondary concerns.

Zumbi, Zion I

The flow comes first, because I don't wanna be a boring MC where it's all about what I'm saying but it doesn't really sound that good. I'm a fan of cats who flow dope and then are saying fresh stuff within it. So I think the flow is what I'm trying to lock in first. The meaning is a close second, but the flow has got to fit first.[52]

Reading rap as poetry places a huge emphasis on its content. Although rhythm and rhyme are addressed to some extent in traditional poetic analysis, they don't take into account how the lyrics fit to the beat of the music, which is one of the central aspects of rapping. Poetry's tools for analyzing rhythms are based on reading the poem aloud, while rapping follows the underlying beat of the music—this makes many of poetry's tools redundant as they miss such a key feature.

Esoteric

On [the track] "Daisycutta," I completely formatted the words to fit with the drum pattern, almost to the point where I let the drums choose the words for me—I kept repeating the second to last word of each line to match with the drums.[53]

Because of this, reading rap as if it were poetry unfairly favors artists with complex content, even if their actual music doesn't *sound* particularly accomplished. In contrast, artists who are incredibly skillful with their flow and delivery, and who make music that is highly nuanced, are unfairly penalized when their work is evaluated as poetry, as it may come across as nonsensical, whimsical, and simplistic when it is laid out on the page.

Royce Da 5'9"
[Jay-Z's track] "Money, Cash, Hoes"—the song ain't really about nothing, really he's just rhyming. But the thing that catches your ear is that flow—it's the way he rides the beat that makes me like the song.[54]

Rapping is a lot closer to percussion in many ways—a number of rappers say they see themselves as percussionists on a track, using words and syllables as if they were individual drum hits. As with percussion, rapping follows the beat of the music.

Tech N9ne
Having the rhythm to being able to stay on beat, it made me sort of like a percussionist. I always wanted to play drums, so if you listen to my flow it's like I'm beating on bongos or something.[55]

Shock G, Digital Underground
I hear and remember the word positions like percussion parts in my head.[56]

The standard form of rap notation is the *flow diagram*—these are diagrams that allow rappers to align their lyrics with the beat of the music. They clearly and accurately represent the rhythms, the rhyme schemes, and the placement of rhymes in ways that cannot be achieved with traditional poetic analyses.

Del the Funky Homosapien
Music theory has helped tremendously. [I use] basic music transcribing, some staff paper, and [I'm] just writing out

the rhythm of the flow, basically. Even if it's just slashes to represent the beats, that's enough to give me a visual path.[57]

Flow diagrams are also used by hip-hop scholars and musicologists to fully explain all of rapping's techniques. They feature extensively in books such as *Rap Music and the Poetics of Identity*,[58] *How to Rap*,[59] *How to Rap 2*,[60] as well as in academic articles such as "On the Metrical Techniques of Flow in Rap Music."[61]

PART II

INFLUENCERS

4. Influential Rappers

The following are key rappers who have been widely influential—creating and developing the techniques that the majority of later rappers use. Therefore this not a "best of all time" list (though all of these artists could arguably be on such a list), but a list of those who have made hugely significant contributions to the art form of rapping. Through these influential figures, you can get a picture of how the craft was created—how more simplistic techniques were developed into complex forms.

"Waves" of Rappers

There are essentially three waves of rapping and rappers. The first laid the foundations during the old school in the early 1970s to 1984 (see p. 133 for more on this era), the second developed and perfected the techniques in hip-hop's golden age of 1986 to 1994 (see p. 147), and the third wave from 1995 onwards use the techniques that have already been created.

The rappers in this chapter are from the first two waves, as these are the eras when the majority of the innovation took place, influencing everything that came after. While there are many very

skillful rappers from the third wave, they mainly use the core techniques that were developed in the previous two waves, with only
occasional additional innovations.

Wave 1: The Foundation (old-school rappers, early 1970s to 1984)

There are three main foundational rappers from the old school:
Melle Mel (of Grandmaster Flash and the Furious Five), Grand-
master Caz (of the Cold Crush Brothers), and Kool Moe Dee (of
Spoonie Gee and the Treacherous Three).

Doug E. Fresh

I mean for me, man, the three best MCs of all time is
Melle Mel, Kool Moe Dee, and Grandmaster Caz. Hands
down, as far as foundation. I know all their rhymes. . . .
The funny thing is, each one of their styles are very different, like Moe Dee was technically extreme, I mean like
sharp, and then slickness and flavor was Caz, [and] Melle
Mel was spiritual.[1]

These three are the most studied of the old-school rappers, especially by the rappers who later developed and mastered rapping's
more advanced techniques. They are often mentioned together
when artists from the golden age talk about their influences.

Rakim

I knew that Melle Mel and Caz and Moe always put something into their work, and every time I sat down to write a
rhyme I always wanted to make sense and show that I went
to school and I took language and social studies and that I
knew how to write a book report. That's the way I took my

rhymes, because of those guys. Listening to them coming up was the best thing that could have happened to me.[2]

Kool G Rap also mentions this trio of old-school rappers together, along with his personal mentor, Silver Fox.

Kool G Rap

I'm a student of the Grandmaster Cazs, the Melle Mels, the Kool Moe Dees, Silver Fox from Fantasy 3 . . . so when people took to me, they were really taking to a part of each of those rappers, because that's where G Rap was branded from. These were the dudes that influenced G Rap to rap the way he raps or to even just have the motivation to want to stand out from everybody else and not only be different but be the best at what I do—it was inspired by those rappers.[3]

Melle Mel

Melle Mel was arguably hip-hop's first elite rapper and became prominent around 1978, before rapping had started to appear on records. Other old-school rappers note that Melle Mel was responsible for changing rapping from simple call-and-response chants spoken over the music to the "on-the-beat" and "in-time-with-the-music" rapping style that became the basis for everyone else— where the focus was more on the lyrics rather than just getting a crowd hyped up with basic chants or talking.

Kool Moe Dee

When you talk about Melle Mel, you're talking about . . . a series of firsts. First of all, he's the first MC to explode in a new rhyme cadence, and change the way every MC rhymed forever. . . . Melle Mel's [on-the-beat] cadence is still the rhyme foundation all MCs are building on. Mel flipped the cadence from the simplistic call-and-response style, and added a rhythmic rhyme punch-line style.[4]

Kid Creole, Grandmaster Flash and the Furious Five

[Our DJ, Grandmaster] Flash, would have guys on the microphone who'd just get on there and say his name, haphazard, no real talent being displayed. And my brother [Melle Mel] . . . I don't know, somehow or another he got in his head that he was going to try to make up his own rhymes, and that's what he did. There was no real outside force that made us write rhymes, because nobody was writing rhymes. [Earlier rappers], they said phrases; they didn't say rhymes. They would say, "On down to the last stop." "More than what you paid at the door." Stuff like that. And when we started writing rhymes, we put sentences together.[5]

When rap began being recorded and released on record labels, Melle Mel brought in political content with "The Message" in 1982 and "White Lines" in 1983 (both under the group name Grandmaster Flash and the Furious Five), at a time when rap was mostly party content and braggadocio.

DJ Premier

Melle Mel from the Furious Five—he was one of the first MCs to take it from just a party atmosphere and talk about what's really going on in the world. And how fucked up New York is and what they see in their hood, and you still can dance to it. To this day when "The Message" comes on you can dance to it, but still the lyrics were incredible, plus he was just an ill performer. Melle Mel, man, he's a beast. He should be given some type of award.[6]

Rakim

Mel, he was like a street poet then, like the way he seen what was going on in the inner city, from "White Lines" to "it's like a jungle. . . ." Melle Mel was the conscious rapper then, from political, to what he seen going on in the neighborhood.[7]

Melle Mel's voice is still one of the most commanding and unique in hip-hop and he had a high level of precision with his rhythm and timing in an era when a lot of other rappers often had a looser, more casual approach to their delivery.

Chuck D, Public Enemy

I liked the guys with the great voices, guys like Melle Mel—I thought they were unbelievable.[8]

Rakim

Melle Mel was like the lion of the game, the lion's roar.[9]

Melle Mel is one of the best examples of the original style of rapping and the fundamental techniques, such as staying on beat, projecting the vocals, and rhyming words while still conveying a strong message. "The Message" is his most famous track, though the majority of his old-school records are great examples of an early innovator and master.

Rakim

Melle Mel was always using big words and ill rhythms, but he'd break it down and get a little political, too, like "White Lines" or the joint he did on *Beat Street*. He was scientifical with it.[10]

Kool Moe Dee

Kool Moe Dee was a member of the old-school rap group Treacherous Three and is primarily known for his intricate rapping style. Of the three key figures of old-school rap, Kool Moe Dee was the one who focused the most on pushing forward the technical aspects of rapping, coming up with more sophisticated rhythms and rhyme schemes. He helped introduce fast rapping on Treacherous Three's song "The New Rap Language."

Special K, Treacherous Three

One day Moe had said this fast rhyme . . . he invented that, I got to give him credit for that.[11]

By laying the groundwork in the old school for later rhyme technicians such as Kool G Rap and Big Daddy Kane to build on, Kool Moe Dee's early innovations set the stage for further developments in intricate rap writing and delivery.

Big Daddy Kane

There were great lyricists before [the golden age rappers]. I don't know if you've heard any of the Kool Moe Dee stuff when he was with the Treacherous Three, but Kool Moe Dee was an incredible MC, early '80s, late '70s. It's like when you listen to Rakim, you can hear a heavy Kool Moe Dee influence.[12]

Many MCs admire the level of sophistication he brought to rapping, noting that he drew from his college education to broaden rap's vocabulary and word play.

Percee P

[Kool Moe Dee] was very influential on me. Back in those times—the vocab and all that, the big words. Treacherous Three tapes, listening to them . . . coming out as an artist, that just inspired me a lot.[13]

Rakim

From Kool Moe Dee, you got the ferocious type of style, but at the same time he was a conscious cat. Moe Dee went to college and kinda incorporated what he was learning in college into his songs. You could tell right away by listening to his metaphors, listening to his four-five-syllable words, and the way he put things together.[14]

DJ Easy Lee, Treacherous Three

He was one of the earliest rappers to have a college degree, so he was well spoken and very articulate.[15]

Moe Dee was also one of the few old-school rappers who had significant success going into the golden age of hip-hop as a solo artist. This later success was helped by his proficiency as a battle rapper—he was involved in some of the most famous battles in hip-hop history, including a live battle with Busy Bee that was widely circulated as a tape recording in the early 1980s, and a battle with LL Cool J over the course of several records during the late 1980s.

DJ Premier

I love Kool Moe Dee, I think he's amazing because he actually made the [rap] battle become what it is, because he took battling to such a whole different level. And he's such a lyrical beast.[16]

Pete Rock
As far as MCs are concerned, Kool Moe Dee was like the top dog at that time. Those infamous rap battles he used to have with Busy Bee were enormous to me when I was young.[17]

Rakim
He was a beast too, I'm sure everybody heard the Busy Bee and Moe Dee battle. Moe Dee kinda enforced that ferocious type of MCing.[18]

Grandmaster Caz

A member of the Cold Crush Brothers, Grandmaster Caz completes the trio of early rappers who set the foundation. Out of the old-school rappers, his legacy is one of the hardest to get to grips with, mainly because there aren't many official recordings by him or the Cold Crush Brothers during their most prominent period.

Many '80s and early '90s rappers listened to bootlegged tapes of live recordings from the Cold Crush Brothers in order to study Caz's techniques—he was particularly influential in shaping how group routines were written (where multiple rappers rap back-and-forth together), a skill later built upon by Run-D.M.C. One of the best places to witness Caz and the Cold Crush Brothers in action is on the 1983 *Wild Style* film, as there is limited access to other recordings.

Kool Moe Dee
There were tapes being made . . . Cold Crush is legendary for their tape sales. With those tapes, 90 percent of the MCs that came from the mid '80s, early '90s studied the

Cold Crush. They studied the old school MCs. Caz definitely, without question, being the lead man [of the Cold
Crush Brothers] and the point man in the equation,
was like the prototype for all of the studying that was going on.[19]

DMC, Run-D.M.C.

Somebody will sneak a tape in or somebody will get a tape
up in the DJ booth and you make the tape, you tape the
show and bring it out in the streets, sell it six to ten dollars—a
lot of tapes were sold like that. My first tape I bought was
the Cold Crush tape, six dollars I paid for it, and it was like
an album to me.[20]

Some of his most famous and quoted lyrics were infamously un-
credited and used by Sugarhill Gang's Big Bank Hank on "Rapper's
Delight," one of the very first and most influential rap recordings.
For many later rappers, "Rapper's Delight" was one of the first
records that they heard with rapping, and so Caz's influence can
also be felt through that record—whether listeners knew it was
partially written by him or not.

He is named by many golden age rappers as a direct major
influence—Rakim, Kool G Rap, and Big Daddy Kane specifically
mention listening to Caz to help develop their styles.

Big Daddy Kane

The flow that I use, I really developed my rap style in the
mid-'80s based on Grandmaster Caz from the Cold Crush
Brothers, from listening to him. That's like really who I
pretty much patterned my style from, and I just took it to
another level once I had the opportunity to get out amongst
the world myself.[21]

Rakim

I'd also make sure I always saw the Cold Crush Brothers. [Grandmaster] Caz was a big influence on me.[22] Grandmaster Caz was like one of the wittiest cats that I heard. His stories and his rhyme style . . . you sat there and you would say, "yo, this kid is nice," but at the same time you had a little smile on your face 'cause half the things he was talking about was half the things you wanted to do and half the things you wanted to be. So Grandmaster Caz, he was just a witty cat and you could tell sometimes when he's rhyming, he's got a smile on *his* face, so he just kinda made rap feel good.[23]

Wave 2: Development and Mastery (golden age rappers, 1986-1994)

The second wave of rappers are from hip-hop's golden age (1986–1994). These four rappers made huge strides forward in developing and perfecting rapping techniques: Rakim (of Eric B. & Rakim), Big Daddy Kane (of the Juice Crew), Kool G Rap (of the Juice Crew), and KRS-One (of Boogie Down Productions).

As with the three foundational, old-school rappers, the four of them are often grouped together when later rappers are discussing their influences.

Rock, Heltah Skeltah

Kool G Rap, Big Daddy Kane, Rakim, KRS-One . . . was basically what shaped my shit when I was young.[24]

Tajai, Souls of Mischief

I grew up in the era where the best guys were like Big Daddy Kane, Kool G Rap, and Rakim—those dudes where you can't listen to their rap once and figure out what they're saying.[25]

Rah Digga
I studied KRS-One, Rakim. . . . Kool G Rap from the Juice Crew kind of set the standards for me as far as what was considered a dope verse and dope rhyming. . . . I just kind of analyzed their styles.[26]

RZA, Wu-Tang Clan
Rakim, Kool G Rap, Kane—I've listened to them since day one, I've met them, and they're exceptional MCs. I mean, *exceptional* MCs.[27] In the old days you always used to argue who was better—Big Daddy Kane, Rakim, or Kool G Rap.[28]

Havoc, Mobb Deep
I learned how to rap just copying from the styles of the artists that was out back then—Big Daddy Kane, Kool G Rap, Rakim, stuff like that. I used to memorize their stuff and try to get a style—like, form a technique—see how their technique was.[29]

MC Serch
I think everyone as a writer who came up in the '80s was influenced in some way, shape, or form by Rakim—[and] I definitely appreciated Big Daddy Kane, Kool G Rap. . . . Those were a lot of my early influences.[30]

The four rappers themselves also often mention each other when they talk about influential and innovative rappers of the golden age.

Big Daddy Kane

I come from where you're hearing cats like Kool G Rap, KRS-One, Rakim—you're hearing a lot of rappers that's spitting hard, so it's like you gotta stay on top of your toes because there's a lot of competition.[31]

Kool G Rap

Being from the era that I'm from, you had to really stand your ground as far as this lyric shit, and that's why that era bred rappers like a Big Daddy Kane, a KRS-One, a Rakim. . . . These dudes, they moved you—they moved you from the soul. Their rapping capability and ability— these dudes were phenomenal.[32]

Rakim

The Juice Crew guys kept me on my toes. When you hear some hot shit, like what Kane and G Rap was doing back then, you can't wait to go home and try to top it.[33]

Since the end of the golden age, around 1994, rappers have mostly employed different combinations of the techniques mastered during this time. That's not to say that there haven't been any innovations from 1995 onwards, but the bulk of the development was done during the golden age, hence why the following rappers are so influential. It is difficult to do any rapping without using something that they either pioneered or perfected.

Rakim

Rakim is often named as the best rapper of all time, based on his monumental impact on the techniques of rapping in 1986. Rappers before Rakim mainly used similar old-school flows—Rakim changed and updated the entire style of rapping, so that the previous style sounded simplistic and outdated. Most rapping recorded after Rakim's debut in 1986 owes a debt to Rakim.

Kool Moe Dee

I would venture to say that Rakim is the most studied MC ever. Any MC that came after 1986 had to study Rakim just to know what to be able to do. As Michael Jordan is the basketball player's basketball player, Rakim is the MCs MC.[34]

Rakim changed the "flow" of rapping—the rhythms and the rhyme schemes. His rhythms were more intricate and have been compared to jazz saxophone improvisation, rather than the more sing-songy, basic rhythms of previous rappers.

Rakim

I ain't played [the saxophone] in a couple of years, but I think that had a lot to do with my rhyme flow. Playing the sax and then enjoying jazz music, man. It's like I learned how to find words inside of the beat. The syncopation and the pauses is all from knowing music, playing the saxophone, listening to John Coltrane and Thelonius Monk and the crazy shit they were doing. I just tried to incorporate that into my rhyme flow. That played a big part in my flow.[35]

His rhyme schemes were more complex, rhyming several times inside the bars of music, rather than using one simple rhyme near the end of each bar like most of his predecessors.

Masta Ace

I remember when Rakim came out—that was like a big moment. Up until [Rakim], everybody who you heard rhyme, the last word in the sentence was the rhyming [word], the connection word. Then Rakim showed us that you could put rhymes within a rhyme, so you could put more than one word in a line that rhymed together.[36]

Rakim

Back in the day I would split the paper with two lines down the middle of the paper, which left me with three sections. I would rhyme in all three sections in every bar. So not only was I rhyming at the end, I was rhyming on the first part of the rhyme, the middle part of the rhyme and the second part of the rhyme. Then when the second bar come, the words would rhyme with the first part of the bar before that, and the middle would rhyme with the middle. This is how I started creating different styles and different rhyme forms and shit like that. I've done so many joints like that I don't even have to split the paper any more. It became like just knowing what I had to do. If I spit this on this bar I know what I had to do on the second bar to make it rhyme. That's how I started creating styles, man, just drawing lines on the paper and putting rhymes in each section.[37]

He also took the delivery (how a rapper uses his/her voice) and the content in different directions as well, using a laid-back conversational tone instead of the louder party voice most rappers had used previously. He focused on witty wordplay and clever uses of language and really put the focus on expanding what could be done with rapping.

Jay-Z

Among New York MCs there was no one like Rakim. In Rakim, we recognized a poet and deep thinker, someone who was getting closer to reflecting the truth of our lives in his tone and spirit. His flow was complex and his voice was ill; his vocal cords carried their own reverb, like he'd swallowed an amp. Back in 1986, when other MCs were still doing party rhymes, he was dead serious. . . . He was approaching rap like literature, like art. And the songs still banged at parties.[38]

Bill Adler

I always saw Rakim as a kind of king of the cosmos. A kind of cosmic sound ruler on the same level as an artist like Jimi Hendrix. [Rakim] was unique for his time because of his coolness. With the possible exception of Spoonie Gee, all the other rappers were shouters. In the jazz sense, Louis Armstrong was a shouter and Lester Young and Miles Davis were cool. [Rakim] was cool like that.[39]

It can be hard to appreciate his impact today, as listeners are so used to hearing this more sophisticated type of rapping. To get a sense of the significance of his debut, it can be helpful to listen to some of the earlier rap recordings, such as Sugarhill Gang's "Rapper's Delight" and Grandmaster Flash and the Furious Five's "The Message." Imagine how back then *all* rapping had that similar sound—the sing-songy, party flow with the big, loudly projected voices and sparsely rapped rhythms.

Kool G Rap

If you had any kind of futuristic flow in comparison to the times back then, it probably wouldn't even be that noticeable now. You'd have to saturate yourself in the music that was going on then to hear the difference.[40]

Then listen to Rakim's style on "My Melody" (under the group name Eric B. & Rakim)—notice how his delivery is a lot more conversational, and how the rhythms aren't as easy to predict as those on the old-school songs. Remember that this new style is in the context of there only ever being the simpler style up until this point—this will give insight into how important Rakim is to rapping.

Grandmaster Flash

Rakim brought so much new thought and technique to the game when he rhymed, it was like he single-handedly reinvented the art form of being an MC. Rakim was doing for rapping what I had done for DJing; he saw the limits of what was out there and figured he could do more.[41]

Kool G Rap

While Rakim is known for influencing almost everyone after him, either directly or indirectly, Kool G Rap (of the hip-hop collective the Juice Crew) is often noted for specifically influencing the most complex rappers who came after him, due to his intricate style of rhyming.

Kool Moe Dee

Kool G Rap is the progenitor and prototype for Biggie, Jay-Z, Treach [of Naughty By Nature], Nore, Fat Joe, Big Pun, and about twenty-five more hard-core MCs. And if you go back and listen, you'll see that he's truly the most lyrical of them all. . . . He made records for the streets, but because he was so lyrical, only future MCs and lyrical junkies could really appreciate what he was doing. He never chose the commercially musical tracks, or made the types of records that would have gotten him any type of airplay.[42]

Nas

Kool G Rap is a major influence. What he did with rapping was he took the lyric level to the highest level it can go. Rakim was scientific, Big Daddy Kane was acrobatic, but Kool G Rap was bloody chainsaws fighting each other lyric style. He took it to a level where it can't go no further. He took it to the highest level.[43]

One of his main focuses was on continually advancing "compound rhymes," which are rhymes with more than one syllable, such as "random luck" rhyming with "vans and trucks." He gradually made this the main trademark of his flow as he advanced compound rhyming from 1986 through to the mid-1990s. The only thing halting any further advancement of the technique was that by this time all of his bars of lyrics were entirely full with rhyming words, taking it to its inevitable limit.

Kool G Rap

[With] multisyllable rhyming, it's not like you're just rhyming *fight* and then *light* and then "with all my *might*." You're rapping *random luck* with *handsome fuck*, "we cop *vans and trucks*"—it be shit like that. It ain't just doing the basics, because that's not ear catching—[more basic rhymes] don't catch the ear like that.[44]

Many rappers, such as Jay-Z, Eminem, and Big Pun, pay homage to the work Kool G Rap did during the golden age of hip-hop. Most of the more complex rappers today use compound rhymes, as it is a technique that immediately signals an advanced rapping style.

Termanology

What I try to do is I try to rhyme two words every bar, it's a lot harder—you're actually writing double the rhymes. There's only a few rappers that really can rap like that, like Kool G Rap.[45]

As well as his influence on rhyming, he was one of the pioneers of more gritty, realistic portrayals of street life, such as on "Streets of New York" in 1990, and introducing Mafioso content into his raps, several years before albums like Raekwon's *Only Built 4 Cuban Linx* made Mafioso themes widely popular in 1995. Even when adopting a hard-core, gangster image, the focus was always primarily on the high calibre of rapping rather than on the image, unlike a lot of rappers who followed in his footsteps.

Raekwon, Wu-Tang Clan

When I think about me being in the street all my life and listening to Kool G Rap: "In the streets of New York, dope fiends leaning from morphine," it was like he was talking to me. It was like he was talking to me personally and talking to the world from our perspective and where we was at.[46]

Kool G Rap

The only [rapper] that came close to being blatant street before me was Melle Mel when he did "The Message," because that was kinda hardcore right there. But he didn't run with that style. When I caught it, I ran with it. Right after "Riker's Island," I did "Road to the Riches." The next album I did "Streets of New York." What's more blatant than that? And to this day street rap is what rules. Everyone says you gotta make commercial songs, [but] those songs are street commercial songs. All 50 [Cent]'s shit is some street shit, [Jay-Z]'s shit was some street shit, Biggie's shit was some street shit—they just learned how to do it in a commercial manner. It's that particular style of rap that rules to this day and in my opinion it's always gonna rule.[47]

Big Daddy Kane

Another member of the Juice Crew, alongside Kool G Rap, was Big Daddy Kane. Kane made similar advances in rhyme as Kool G Rap during the same period of time (they would often rap over the phone to each other in friendly competition), and he experienced more commercial success—because of this he is generally more widely known than Kool G Rap.

Big Daddy Kane

Me and [Kool] G Rap had a competitive relationship, but it was for the best. It was the type of thing where we'd talk on the phone at night and G would be like, "I got this joint," and he'd kick it and I'd go, "Aight, I got something." When we hang up the phone we [were] like, "Damn, he came hard," and we [went] back to the pen and paper. We always had love for each other. For me there was always a certain way I felt about G—I always feel like I took his slot. I always felt he never got the props he deserved. When I took off it wasn't really room for two, so my man never got to shine the way I know he could have. I don't think the world really knows how great [Kool G Rap] is on the mic.[48]

Big Daddy Kane was one of the first rappers to introduce the smooth, ladies' man persona, though with an emphasis on the rapping technique first and the image second. He mixed this with witty battle-rap punchlines and a sarcastic, condescending tone. His vocal delivery is also one of the most revered in hip-hop—a smooth baritone comparable to Rakim's.

Jay-Z

[Big Daddy] Kane was playing a role, hip-hop's first playboy: He had the silk robes and pretty girls in all his videos, all that. But his flow was sick. . . . He was condensing, stacking rhymes one on top of another. Trying to keep up with him was an exercise in breath control, in wordplay, in speed and imagination. He was relentless on the mic.[49]

RZA, Wu-Tang Clan

Big Daddy Kane was one of the first MCs with swagger. This dude had the Brooklyn aggressiveness and yet he still has all the girls on him and he still had hardcore styles.[50]

Kane is often placed in lists of the top five rappers ever, as he is one of the most studied lyricists of the golden age—named by many of the next generation as an artist whose records taught them how to rap. Also noteworthy is his ghostwriting for other artists, such as Biz Markie and Roxanne Shanté, and his versatility in being able to write in different styles to suit their personas.

Ice-T

To me, Big Daddy Kane is still today one of the best rappers. I would put Big Daddy Kane against any rapper in a battle. Jay-Z, Nas, Eminem, any of them. I could take [his song] "Raw" right now and put it up against any record [from today]. Kane is one of the most incredible lyricists . . . Big Daddy Kane can rap circles around cats.[51]

KRS-One

KRS-One, formerly of the group Boogie Down Productions, is known as an incredible live MC, with the levels of outstanding enunciation, timing, vocal presence, and energy needed for live performance.

O.C., Diggin' in the Crates
Probably the first thing I learned in MCing is breath control, I learned that from KRS. I seen him do a show one time—I seen him rock for two hours that night. He had his hype man or whatever, but for the most part I never seen nothing like that. Like, damn, this dude sounds like his records or better.[52]

On his records, his subject matter often aims to educate listeners, introducing them to political and historical issues and events, as well as the promotion of socially aware hip-hop in general.

Grandmaster Flash
KRS was also telling people things nobody else did: don't smoke crack, stop making babies, stop committing black-on-black violence . . . know your history. It all seemed so obvious, but it took on a new meaning coming through the speakerbox on the radio. Now the Bronx had a rapper who told it like it was. KRS wasn't a braggart about anything other than the knowledge he had to teach.[53]

Through his flow, he helped to introduce a lot of new varied rhythms, sometimes borrowed from reggae and ragga MCing. His records are often exciting and unpredictable to listen to because of this, with numerous changes in the flow throughout his songs—this paved the way for later rappers with rapid-fire, alternating flows, such as the groups Das EFX and Fu-Schnickens.

Kool Moe Dee

[KRS-One] is one of the more versatile MCs in the game. I think he has more styles than anybody, period . . . [he has] more flows than anybody I have ever heard.[54]

KRS-One is also known as one of the premier battle rappers, due to his live performance skills, his ability to improvise lyrics off the top of his head, and his knowledge of a wide array of rapping styles.

Jadakiss

[KRS-One] was dropping knowledge and it was still hard. That's incredibly hard to do: to get accepted, to get your point across and be looked at like an incredible lyricist and stage performer. He covered everything. His stage show is crazy, freestyle is crazy. He can get deep on you. His battle raps are crazy. He was the teacher. He was dangerous.[55]

5. Influential Beatmakers

As with rapping, beatmaking can also be broken down into three waves—the first as the foundation, the second developing and perfecting the techniques, and the third using the techniques that have already been created.

However, beatmaking differs slightly from rapping in how the techniques are usually passed along. Most rappers develop their skills by listening to other rappers on records, repeating their lyrics, and then writing their own raps based on the techniques they've heard and consistently repeated.

Sean Price, Heltah Skeltah
Back in the days, I would listen to [hip-hop radio shows], that was my teacher, them shows, that's how I learned how to rap—just listening. I was a fan of it and wanted to be a part of it.[1]

Brother Ali
I learned how to rap from listening and memorizing the people in the mid-'80s, people like Melle Mel and Slick

Rick and UTFO and Whodini and Run-D.M.C. I learned from memorizing their things and rapping like that.[2]

Yukmouth, The Luniz

I picked up the skills from listening to rap. What really made me rap was listening to Kool G Rap, KRS-One, N.W.A., Geto Boys—that combination made my rap style, and Big Daddy Kane. So when them albums came out I would learn their raps and then I started writing my own raps and that's how I basically started.[3]

With beatmaking, there are some aspects that can be picked up from listening, but there are also many methods that are mainly passed from one beatmaker to the next, in person. So rather than everyone pointing to the same group of influential artists, as rappers do, beatmakers often have a more personal connection to the people who inspired them—their mentors are often people they know personally, who showed them how to use a particular piece of equipment or showed them a certain record to sample. In some cases there is even a chain, whereby one person taught another, and that second person went on to teach several other people.

Mr. Walt, Da Beatminerz

You've heard of the game "Six Degrees of Kevin Bacon"? In the [producing] game there's a six degrees of separation from Large Professor. Somehow, Large Professor taught you [how to use] the SP-1200, even if he physically never taught you the SP. And I would tell people: yo, I had my SP training [via] Large Professor. Because Large Professor taught Q-Tip [and] Q-Tip taught me the SP-12.[4]

DJ Premier

Showbiz taught me that. Showbiz, from Showbiz and AG.
I gotta give him credit. He's the one that taught me how to
chop [up samples]. I learned about filtering from Large
Professor. . . . [Showbiz has] got mad records, and he's like,
"Yo, take whatever you want." We can borrow each other's
records. Like when I did "Can't Stop the Prophet," for Jeru
[the Damaja, Showbiz] gave me the "Shingaling" drums.[5]

Wave 1: The Foundation (pre-golden age beatmakers, 1979-1986)

Due to the way information is passed down, early beatmakers are
not as clearly cited as influencers and pioneers by later beatmakers
as early rappers are with later rappers. Despite this complication,
there are still three beatmakers who do stand out due to their contributions in shaping the early sound of hip-hop beatmaking. They
are Clifton "Jiggs" Chase, Larry Smith, and Kurtis Mantronik.

These three laid a lot of the groundwork that later beatmakers
would build on, and they were pioneers in using the ever-advancing
studio technology of the time, as well as in the styles that they
brought to hip-hop.

Clifton "Jiggs" Chase

Sugar Hill Records was the first major hip-hop label in the late
'70s and early '80s, and Clifton "Jiggs" Chase was their in-house
producer and arranger. Most of the very first hip-hop records
people heard had his production sound and they were often based
on funk and disco loops replayed by the house band.

Keith Leblanc

Back then, playing live in the studio was normal. The arranger Clifton "Jiggs" Chase would get with the rappers and do an arrangement based on what they wanted to use and then make up a chart. Then we'd add things. The musical ethic was really good at that time. You had to get it right or there'd be someone else in there recording the next day. We'd cut a track on the Friday, drive home to Connecticut, drive back to New Jersey on the Monday and hear the track on the radio. A lot of the time, we were playing maybe a bar of someone else's music. So we wanted to cut it better than the original![6]

Later songs on Sugar Hill Records started to employ more electronic elements such as drum machine programming, as on Grandmaster Flash and the Furious Five's "The Message," and this helped hip-hop to embrace the new production technology which would soon replace the studio musicians. Although Sugar Hill Records's percussionist, Duke Bootee, wrote the majority of "The Message," he credits Jiggs as the producer who taught him drum machine programming (along with the in-house drummer, Keith Leblanc).

Duke Bootee

I got the gig [as Sugar Hill Records's percussionist] through Jiggs Chase, who I used to play jazz with back in the days. He was my mentor. All those Sugar Hill records will say "Jigsaw Productions"—that's Jiggs Chase. He brought me in, and the first record that I played on was "Freedom" by Grandmaster Flash & The Furious 5, I played congas and timbales on that. Then I played on every Sugar Hill track after that, all the timbales, congas, and vibes are me. We all came up in cover bands so we could play exactly like the original, and sometimes make it a little better ... we prided ourselves on playing shit better than the original record. [Jiggs] plays keyboards, programs drums . . . [I learned to program drums on a drum machine] from Keith and Jiggs, they were at the forefront of that.[7]

Larry Smith

Larry Smith helped to completely change the course of hip-hop music when he produced Run DMC's first two albums.

DJ Premier
Larry Smith is a producer that used to work with Kurtis Blow, Run-D.M.C. with "Rock Box" and all that. He did a lot of the Whodini records. Very, very, very good producer.[8]

He initially played a part in popularizing the old school's commercial, disco-infused sound, contributing to popular tracks by Kurtis Blow, such as "The Breaks" and "Christmas Rappin'," in the early '80s. However, it was his production for Run-D.M.C.'s first two albums, filled with raw, sparse drum machine beats, that drew the old-school era to a close and ushered in the new school's harder, more abrasive, street-orientated music in 1984 (see p. 141 for more on this transition).

DMC, Run-D.M.C.
I want the world to know when you talk about the best producers like Jam Master Jay, DJ Premier, Swizz Beatz, and Dr. Dre, you have to add Larry Smith. I feel so bad, because when Run-D.M.C. got inducted into the Rock and Roll Hall of Fame [in 2009] I wanted to take that platform to mention Larry. Because there would be no hip-hop as we know it today if it wasn't for Larry Smith. He did both

of Run-D.M.C.'s first two albums (*Run-D.M.C.*, *King of Rock*), and he did Whodini's biggest singles . . . Come on! Larry Smith's musical arsenal equals Dr. Dre's. I know Jermaine Dupri knows that, because he was touring with Whodini in those days. Think about the body of work that he did. I think Larry's notoriety gets lost because of Rick Rubin. People still think that Rick produced the first two Run-D.M.C. albums. But there would be no *Raising Hell* without those first two albums.[9]

His style was further popularized and built on by other producers such as Rick Rubin, though it was Larry Smith's groundwork that provided hip-hop with its new direction and sound.

Kurtis Mantronik

Kurtis Mantronik, of the group Mantronix, was one of the key pioneers in hip-hop's use of studio technology. Most producers who favor keyboards and drum machines over samples and sampling have been influenced by his intricate and elaborate early work in this area.

Mannie Fresh

My patterns and stuff is based around [Mantronik's music], his energy and that music was just always energy, you know. It was something that always kept the party started and what I totally liked about it, he took the focus off of the MCs, like you could be a horrible MC but if you got one of his beats you could [still have a good record]. Then on top of that, he was one of the dudes that did variety. He did [the production for *Back to the Old School* by] Just-Ice, he did a couple people, he did Joyce Sims. He did R&B as well, he was like one of the first producers that was a hip-hop producer that was doing all of that. [He had a lot of electronic type of sounds . . .] he was one of the very first to really do that.[10]

The first Mantronix LP, *The Album*, is a seminal record that effectively demonstrated what could be done with studio production, leading the way for future producers who would later combine his techniques with samples.

Kurtis Mantronik

I was a nerd and really into technology so I was definitely into the production side from the start. I always used the latest technology . . . I used the [Roland TR-]808 drum machine a lot back then because I just love the bass that it gave.[11]

Wave 2: Expansion and Refinement (golden age beatmakers, 1986-1994)

As with rapping's second wave, innovation in beatmaking grew exponentially during hip-hop's golden age (see p. 147 for more on the golden age). By this time, equipment which could loop and chop up parts of records was becoming more affordable, accessible, and more technologically powerful. Things that were impossible due to technical restraints a few years before soon became standard elements of hip-hop beatmaking.

Four beatmakers are particularly influential from this period: Marley Marl (of the Juice Crew), Paul C., the Bomb Squad (a group of beatmakers), and Prince Paul.

Marley Marl

Prior to Marley Marl, hip-hop records were mainly made by either session musicians replaying disco and funk hits or from the sounds of drum machine programming—where you create a track with pre-recorded drum sounds that come with the drum machine.

There were problems with both these approaches. Using a live band meant you weren't using records and "breaks" as the earlier pioneers of hip-hop had done (see p. 133-135), so the music was often more like disco with rapping over it, rather than its own, new genre. And using drum machine sounds meant you were limited to the default sounds that came with the machine—these were often more electronic and "thin" sounding, rather than the soulful, "big" sound of drum breaks on records.

Marley Marl brought in a whole new way of creating beats, which is the foundation that most hip-hop beatmakers still use today. He discovered that he could sample small, individual parts of a record (usually drum hits, such as the sound of a kick drum or a snare drum), allowing him to program drum patterns with the sounds sampled from records, instead of the stock drum machine sounds.

Evil Dee, Beatminerz
Marley was the dude that started us sampling. Because he discovered sampling by accident. . . . He was sampling some vocals and he sampled a kick or a snare, I think, and that's when he figured out, like, yo, wait a minute, you know what this means?![12]

This meant that instead of using the often tinny and "small" drum hits and sounds from a drum machine, he could take a snare drum sound from a funk record or a kick drum sound from a rock record, for example, and use those sounds to create new drum patterns. This instantly changed the sound of many hip-hop records, as beatmakers now had a huge range of sounds at their disposal— they could use any drums from any record ever made.

Marley Marl

I made a mistake at Unique Recording Studios . . . sampled a snare inside a sampler by mistake when I was trying to get a voice off the record. I started playing the snare along with the track and I asked the engineer, "turn off that [other] snare, that [other] drum kit. That weak-ass, thin drum snare, turn that shit down." Now I'm popping a James Brown snare with my beat I just made, I'm looking at the engineer like, "Yo, dude, you know what this means?" I was like, "I can take any kick, any snare, any hi-hat, and make my own pattern with the drums that I hear on a record? It's crazy!" People didn't find out for like four years what I was doing. Why is his drums sound so crispy? Russell Simmons [of Def Jam Records] and them pulling their brains out trying to [figure it out] . . . cats told me about the sessions, [saying,] yo, Russell's screaming at us, "Why can't you make records like Marley Marl? He's in his living room! You're in a million-dollar studio!"[13]

Marley went on to produce many of the key early golden age releases, with beats based on this new technique, such as records for Eric B. & Rakim (see p. 171) and the Juice Crew, as well as later releases with LL Cool J and KRS-One.

DJ Premier

Marley Marl is my idol of hip-hop. He's like the James Brown of hip-hop.[14]

Paul C.

Now that parts of a record could be sampled and pieced together, beatmakers started taking this further and began honing the techniques. Paul C. was hugely influential in this, creating intricate and seamless "chops." This is where parts of one or several records are "chopped" up into pieces, ready to be sequenced into new patterns with the aid of music production equipment.

CJ Moore

You couldn't get [a sample] into the recording medium unless you chopped it up and put it back together, one bit at a time. For example, you've got a kick from Ohio Players, a snare from James Brown, another snare from Herbie Hancock, a hi-hat from MFSB—you've got different [drum] kits recorded in different rooms at different times on different boards. The challenge was to tie that in together to make it sound like one kit. Make it sound better than it did when it came off the record, which was usually trashed.[15]

Cut Chemist, Jurassic 5

The drum programming on "Snake Eyes," [a song by Main Source, produced by Large Professor who was mentored by Paul C.], that's [the drums from the song] "Synthetic Substitution" chopped up really nice. That's an example of what I think good production is and how I'm influenced— chopped to the point where it doesn't sound chopped. It's totally natural sounding.[16]

Pete Rock

I always listened to [Ultramagnetic MCs'] "Give the Drummer Some," trying to figure it out. I thought maybe [Paul C.]

knew someone at Polygram that had James Brown's reels. There's no way in the world he could sample [Dee Felice] and take the sounds out. Those are the illest drums I ever heard.[17]

A use of the chop that Paul C. developed was to take out unwanted parts of a record. For example, if there was a drum loop with a horn sound you didn't like in the middle of it, you could "remove" the horn sound by cleverly chopping that whole segment of the record into pieces and putting the pieces back together in the right way without the horn.

Large Professor

I saw [Paul C.] chopping up James Brown's "The Chicken" with the horns and shit. And then he starts to play it, but without the horns, and I was like, "Oh shit!"[18]

Paul C. also used a technique where he would "pan" a record to take a sample from just one of the stereo channels (i.e., just the sound coming from the left or right speaker). If there was a record where the drums were recorded on the left channel and the bass was recorded on the right channel, this meant he could take just the drums, without the bass, if he sampled just from the left channel. Using this method, more elements could be sampled more easily—rather than waiting for a part of the record with just drums, you could wait for a part where the drums were only in one channel, even if other sounds were present in the other channel.

Large Professor

[Ultramagnetic MCs' "Give the Drummer Some," from 1988] is early sample innovation. Paul C. was an extreme sound scientist, and this may be the most prime example of his futuristic approach. To take the James Brown "There Was a Time" off the *Gettin' Down to It* album and pan [using only the left or right side of a stereo record] to get only the drums, was unheard of at that time.[19]

Ced Gee, Ultramagnetic MCs

That was one of the things Paul showed me: sometimes the drums would be clean on one channel, so you have to pan the sound. You have to pan the drums on the Dee Felice Trio record to get the sample we used in "Give the Drummer Some." Once we started panning records, it was crazy.[20]

These technical innovations that Paul C. introduced helped beat-makers to better translate the ideas in their heads into actual records and set the stage for many later, notable beatmakers, such as Pete Rock and DJ Premier, both of whom have used chops extensively. He was also a mentor to Large Professor, who passed many of his techniques on to other well-respected beat-makers in person.

Large Professor

That's what Paul C. brought to hip-hop: the chop. You gotta make it do what you want it to do. Pete Rock mastered the chop; he'll make a record go crazy. I love the stabs and programming those little sharp pieces.[21] [Paul C.] just kinda took me under his wing . . . I saw how his shit was set up and everything. He's like, "Yo, press this button and press this button! I'll see you in a minute," then he'd go to sleep and shit! And I'd be sitting there, pressing the buttons! That's how I was taught.[22]

Tragically, Paul C. was murdered in 1989 just as his career was blossoming, but his innovations live on as fundamental, standard techniques used by today's beatmakers.

Domingo

Paul C.'s contribution to late '80's, early '90's hip-hop was crucial to the New York sound. Paul C. was a mentor to many and his production techniques got picked up by many New York producers, including Large Pro, Ced Gee of the Ultra Magnetic MCs, and even myself. I had the honor to work with him a few times. If you don't know who Paul C. McKasty was, then do yourself a favor and [look up] his name. Real hip-hop history right here.[23]

The Bomb Squad

Public Enemy is one of the most acclaimed groups in hip-hop, and a large part of their sound is due to their production crew, the Bomb Squad. The second Public Enemy album in particular, *It Takes a Nation of Millions to Hold Us Back*, is often named as one of the best albums of all time, in any genre (see p. 172).

They pioneered the use of a massive barrage of samples, often discordant and abrasive, to produce a wall of sound—layering samples upon samples and triggering multiple sounds to create musical breakdowns, such as in the middle of the track, "Night of the Living Baseheads." This really opened up producers' imaginations to what could be done with sampling and hip-hop production.

James Lavelle, UNKLE

[Public Enemy's album, *It Takes a Nation of Millions to Hold Us Back*, it was] similar to [the gangsta rap group] N.W.A., it had that power. The production at the time was unreal; Bomb Squad were the best out there. It took hip-hop to a completely new level.[24]

Rather than using a few drum sounds or just a sampled riff from a record as the basis of a song, they often used many small pieces, intricately put together to create a dense soundscape. Due to sampling becoming more expensive and litigious in the 1990s, as older artists realized they could charge more if they were sampled by popular hip-hop artists, the Bomb Squad's early signature sound has been difficult to emulate.

Chuck D, Public Enemy

Public Enemy's music was affected more than anybody's [with the change in the expense of sampling], because we were taking thousands of sounds. If you separated the sounds, they wouldn't have been anything—they were unrecognizable. The sounds were all collaged together to make a sonic wall. Public Enemy was affected because it is too expensive to defend against a claim. So we had to change our whole style, the style of *It Takes a Nation* and *Fear of a Black Planet*, by 1991.[25]

Rather than relying on sparse drum beats or melodic funk, R&B, or disco loops that previous hip-hop usually employed, the Bomb Squad often went for a loud, noisy, unmelodious sound, comparable to certain punk or heavy metal artists.

Hank Shocklee, the Bomb Squad

We didn't want to use anything we considered traditional R&B stuff—bass lines and melodies and chord structures and things of that nature. The sound has a look to me, and Public Enemy was all about having a sound that had its own distinct vision.[26]

MCA, the Beastie Boys

I remember listening to *Nation of Millions* over and over again when it came out, with headphones. That was the first time someone had approached a hip-hop album like other artists—rock artists is what I mean—would approach an album.[27]

Hank Shocklee, the Bomb Squad

If you go back through musical history, anything that was done that pushed the envelope was perceived as noise. Rock 'n' roll was noise. Classical music was noise. We came across with a new form of music—basically taking music that was already pre-recorded and pulling out the frequencies and sustaining them and stretching them and bending them and controlling them in a fashion that felt to us like rock 'n' roll. We took anything and made it feel like a rock guitar, whether it be a horn blast or a violin string pad.[28]

Due to the experimental nature of their way of producing, they were also responsible for new techniques, such as an early form of "filtering," where certain sound frequencies are removed, several years before it became a standard practice.

Hank Shocklee, the Bomb Squad

Now those are presets, [processes that come as standard functions on studio equipment,] but we created those things before all these companies even knew what the hell was going on. When you look at filtering, for example, that was a thing that we were doing because we stumbled across it. It was actually a defect in the original [E-mu] SP-12 design. When you plugged in the plug into the mix out of a SP-12, and the cord doesn't go in all the way, it still makes a connection but it shaves off the high end [sound frequencies]; what was left was the bass portions of the sound. When we realized that we said, "Oh wow, that's a cool effect."[29]

Another innovation of the Bomb Squad was to act like a traditional band, where each member would take charge of a particular sampler (see p. 122) or turntable and they would "jam" and improvise sounds until they came up with something they liked.

Hank Shocklee, the Bomb Squad

We all did everything. Besides me, Keith [Shocklee], Eric [Sadler], and Chuck [D], there was Flavor Flav and Terminator X. Everything was divvied up to whoever was feeling what at that particular moment. If Eric felt like, "I can add a little sequence part here"—it may just be a tambourine loop—then he would add that. If Flav feels like, "I wanna add the timing to this little drum sample," he's going to add that. . . . Nobody had a station, but what we did do is get down as a band. Eric might be on the drum pads, Keith might be on another set of drum pads, Chuck might be on a turntable, Flavor might grab a bass, Terminator was on a turntable, I might be on a keyboard sampler. And we're all just jamming—just making a fucking mess—but we're running tape. Every now and then you'll get a moment that will be the most incredible five seconds and that little piece might end up being a part of a record.[30]

This unique, pioneering way of using studio production equipment resulted in a very distinct, freer, and more organic sound than had previously been made.

Hank Shocklee, the Bomb Squad

We did not sequence things, [with the equipment keeping it in precise time]. We wanted everything to have our feel. If you really listen closely, a lot of the timing on things is not correct and it's not supposed to be correct. You can easily take a high hat, put it into a machine, quantize it [so that it is perfectly in time], and let it run from beginning to end. That sounds very mechanical. You're not going to get the loose feel of it. When we play it by hand, the high hats are at different lengths and different timing. When you start stacking those things, you're getting a groove that's being created from all the things that are a little bit off. The reason why most records made today are boring is because they're linear. They begin and end doing the same patterns, the same spacing, the same timing. Records are supposed to be a living, breathing thing.[31]

Prince Paul

Prince Paul has produced a number of acclaimed releases throughout hip-hop's history—one of his most enduring production projects was De La Soul's debut album, *3 Feet High and Rising*, where he expanded hip-hop's sampling palette considerably by looking to genres and artists outside of hip-hop's usual sphere.

Jaycee, the Aphilliates

When I got *3 Feet High and Rising* I remember listening to it on the bus and thinking, "Damn, they're not using the typical samples that other people are using." A lot of early to mid '80s rap was based on James Brown loops and *Ultimate Breaks and Beats* samples, [which were compilations of mainly funk and R&B tracks]. A lot of Def Jam's sound was ruled by straight Roland TR-808 [drum machine sounds] with samples manually layered on top of it. De La [Soul's record] just didn't sound like anything else, period. I was so impressed with the album that I bought it on all formats: CD, cassette, and [vinyl] LP.[32]

Tom Silverman

That album is so important because it threw out the rule-book. At the time, hip-hop was starting to define itself as being one thing. . . . These guys said: "No, you don't have to sound like that."[33]

Prince Paul

It was a combination of me, [and De La Soul's] Pos, Dave, and Mase. We combined our collections. We more or less gathered what our families listened to and had collected over the years. Pos had a deep collection. His dad had some really obscure records, which helped us out a lot. I'd been collecting forever and I always had weird records. Everybody came to the table with their own little thing. It was almost like we were trying to outdo each other, like, "Oh, look what I got!" That's why the album sounds so layered out. We just kept adding stuff to it. When that album came out we treaded on territory that nobody was willing to go. I just remember people scratching their heads. Either you really liked it or you hated it. It was an extreme record and it was radical in its time.[34]

Prince Paul's methodology of finding samples from unusual sources has had a huge impact on subsequent producers' styles.

RZA, Wu-Tang Clan

When I first started producing, the only person I knew doing the kind of bugged-out sampling I was into was Prince Paul—him and maybe a few other guys. I still think that first De La Soul album, *3 Feet High and Rising*, is a masterpiece. Paul and I have been friends since 1988. He even programmed the hi-hats on my first single on Tommy Boy. I never thought about imitating his style, but he did show everybody that you could take anything with a sampler—cartoons, children's records, French lessons—and make it musical. I'm a kung-fu fiend, so I would sample from kung-fu movies, but also, if I'm walking down the street and see a *Peter Pan* vinyl sitting on the ground, a man selling it for a dollar—I'm buying that. If I see a *Flintstones* record for a dollar—I'm buying that. Anything. I buy it, I listen to it, and start hearing the phrases inside of it. And then, I'm sampling it.[35]

His music also often has a very playful and free approach—unafraid to include "mistakes" and diverge from how hip-hop normally sounds.

Posdnuos, De La Soul

Prince Paul taught us that you need to leave open the surprise of a mistake, because it could turn around and be great, Paul's a genius that way. He's not afraid to scrap a record and start from scratch and try something else totally different. A lot of ideas came from us just joking around. I'd crack a joke and next thing you know we're doing a game show. We learned, mostly from Paul, that you don't always need to map things out. You can make mistakes. And the zaniness of the album, overall, definitely came from Paul.[36]

Prince Paul

There are tons of mistakes on that album. I'll listen to it and go, "Oops. That was a mistake, there's a mistake, that's a mistake." There's a part of "Me, Myself And I" where the music drops out; that was a mistake. Me and Pos used to mix everything by hand. We didn't have automation. Everything was kind of on the fly as the song went along. There was a part where one of us was supposed to leave the beat in, and we forgot. We just looked at each other, threw it back in on time and said, "Eh, that's good enough!"[37]

He has continued this approach of using unusual sounds and sources in his later solo work and production for other hip-hop luminaries, ensuring that hip-hop keeps an "alternative" side to its sound.

James Lavelle, UNKLE

[*3 Feet High and Rising*] was definitely a reaction to the slightly more hardcore area of what was going on in hip-hop. As a concept record, it's probably one of the best ever. It's like the Pink Floyd of hip-hop, their *Dark Side of the Moon*, the way it musically and sonically moves around. . . . It was an interesting contrast from things being much more hardcore and urban . . . it became such a huge influence around what was going on at the time. It broke down a lot of barriers; it crossed into so many different peoples' lives. The samples, the whole way it was put together, it was so unique. An amazing collage; an amazing painting of a record.[38]

6. Hip-Hop Instruments

In the same way that a rock band uses vocals, guitar, bass, and drums, or a jazz band or classical orchestra has a collection of traditional instruments, hip-hop also has its own standard instruments. Some of these create music in real time, such as vocals and DJ scratching and mixing, and some are used in the studio to piece together musical backing tracks. Many of these methods of making music use types of equipment that aren't always associated with the term *instrument*.

RZA, Wu-Tang Clan

A lot of people still don't recognize the sampler as a musical instrument. I can see why. A lot of rap hits over the years used the sampler more like a Xerox machine. If you take four whole bars that are identifiable, you're just biting that shit. But I've always been into using the sampler more like a painter's palette than a Xerox. . . . You listen to a song like "Knowledge God" by Raekwon: It took at least five to seven different records chopped up to make one two-bar phrase. That's how I usually work.[1]

Sometimes the term "instrument" is used only for things that can be played live—the turntable, certain samplers and sequencers such as the MPC, and of course keyboards and vocals, can all be used to produce sounds in real time.

Alchemist

[The MPC is] like an instrument. I know some people who work the machine in a way where on stage . . . it's incredible. There's a lot of other technology that can let you make beats with a computer and stuff, but I think it takes away from the live ability. In general the MPC is an instrument because of what you can do with it. I've seen guys treating it like a turntable. The turntable was made for one thing and you can make creative turntablism out of it. With the MPC there's like a whole style of live entertainment that actually hasn't been fully explored. It's crazy. That's what separates it from a lot of these new things. You can't use your little computer out live and then treat it like an instrument—it's a computer![2]

Vocals/Beatboxing

One of the most central instruments in hip-hop is the voice, even though it is not usually used in the traditional way to hit notes and to sing melodies. A hugely important element of a rapper's style is his or her voice, and many of the most acclaimed and successful hip-hop artists are known for their vocal presence and personality.

Andy Cat, Ugly Duckling

The history of hip-hop is filled with rappers who have distinct voices. In fact, it may be the most important element for a rap vocalist, [as suggested on] Gang Starr's song

"Mostly the Voice," because that's the first thing a listener will hear and identify with.[3]

Brother Ali

So much of it is the voice and feeling of hearing it. [That] adds so much to it that I don't like reducing what I'm saying to writing. I put the lyrics in the little booklet for [one of my albums, but] even just looking at them I'm like, if you've never heard these, if you're only reading them, then I think you're missing a lot of it. It's not just solely the words.[4]

As well as being used for rapping, the voice can also be used to produce hip-hop beats, in the form of beatboxing. This is where a beatboxer will learn to make individual drum sounds vocally, and then perform them in different rhythms, mimicking drumming. Beatboxers often also add sound effects that range from video game sounds to phones ringing, to other instruments such as trumpets and bass guitars.

Rahzel

I love beatboxing. Rhyming is cool, but there are a lot of people rhyming. I figure I'd rather be the big fish in a small pond! I would have to say [one of my biggest influences is virtuoso jazz vocalist] Bobby McFerrin. He's got such class and style. He's on a whole 'nother level, and to me that's the way I strive to be. He's in his own lane and he's my biggest inspiration with regards to his focus and his drive. He motivates me to not conform to the corporate music thing, to not be afraid.[5]

Doug E. Fresh

I would rhyme, but the beatbox would separate me from the rest that much more . . . it was an element of hip-hop that never really existed and I created it. People have toyed around with it—I can never say people hadn't done beats with their mouth—but I can say that the person who coined the phrase "the human beatbox" and took it to the stage and took it in front of people and actually did the beatbox, was me. And that's when you started to have other beatboxers that came out. Kurtis Blow was the producer of the Fat Boys [who also did beatboxing], but he knows that I'm the original because when he was having a problem in Harlem, at 125th Street, because he didn't have no turntables, he asked me if I wanted to get up and do the beatbox for him while he rhymed. I did the beatbox, and that was history right there.[6]

Records

Records, whether albums, singles, or EPs, are the raw material of hip-hop music creation. As shown in chapter 7 (p. 133), the music was first created around "breaks" from many different records. Going out and finding these records is known as record "digging."

Pete Rock
I'm a fiend, it's like being a drug addict with records! I can't stop buying them, I love to dig and find new things and even to this day I'm like a big kid with it. And I enjoy listening to these albums, not just to sample, but just to hear, maybe there's something still there that I can learn.[7]

Most record diggers are looking for vinyl records, often because of the warmer, grittier sound associated with them. As vinyl records usually have label artwork on the record itself, as well as a lot of information on their large album covers, this meant that hip-hop producers had different ways of learning about music than today's audiences, who may have no idea what label, producer, or specific musicians made the music they listen to.

DJ Premier

Motown records always said a "Jobete" company, so I was like, [let me find] everything that says Jobete. The Stevie Wonder records, Gladys Knight and the Pips, the Temptations, the Jackson 5, Diana Ross and the Supremes . . . it always said Jobete. And then you'd look at the back of that album and it had the year, 1971 [for example]. And then the Jackson 5 records sounded like the way the label looked . . . when you'd see the blue map of Detroit, Motown spinning around, it always sounded good, [so you made a connection between the sound and the label artwork]. All of that is turning in your head, to wonder, "how does this get put together?" And I'm seeing "produced by" and I'm like, "wow, that same person did that record, his name's on that," so I'm like, "if their name is on that, that means it's going to be good again!" [As a kid] I'd go right to the soul section and look for anything that had Jobete or Motown on it or Atlantic. Wilson Pickett was on Atlantic . . . Atlantic had the funny little curl on the A . . . I want anything that says Atlantic on it.[8]

Pete Rock

I came across a couple of labels . . . that intrigued me: Sussex, Buddah Records, Curtom Records, Polydor, Fantasy Records, Spring Records, to go over to the jazz side, you had Columbia, you had Blue Note. So many of these labels made my eyes pop, like wow, and then you'd hear the sounds coming from these records like, oh my gosh, who produced this? And you'll look on the back and see all the credits and then the personnel of the band members. . . . [You would listen for] what sound intrigued you the most, [like] the bass line. I used to love bass lines, so I would look and see someone like a Jim Hall on bass, he played with Ron Carter. Then you had Curtis Mayfield's bass player, he was the ultimate, he played on a lot of Curtis Mayfield's songs. That, to me, was a learning experience, looking on the back of these records and then looking at the distributor who actually made the label or who the president of the label was, things like that, I was into all of that.[9]

Hip-hop beatmakers will often have favorite digging spots—record stores that sell a lot of the genre or obscure records that they like to find and sample.

RZA, Wu-Tang Clan

In New York City, the Village was the place to find your ill records. That, or you could go to Beat Street Rock 'n' Soul. And on West Forty-third in Times Square, you had the Music Factory. It doesn't exist anymore, but that was the hip-hop spot. That's where you could find every break beat, every dope hook, all types of funk. When I found that store, I just went crazy. I'm like that even now with records. Once Wu-Tang went on tour, while other guys went chasing girls, I'd just go record shopping. I bought a lot of records out in Switzerland, France, all over the world. I dropped ten grand in Switzerland on one trip, just on records. I got the record I used in "Gravel Pit" in France, when I was living there in a villa in 1998. That's from a French film soundtrack for the movie *Belphegor*—that Antoine Duhamel shit.[10]

Beatmakers are often careful about how they store and treat their records, as the records are such an integral part of the music they make.

Large Professor

The most important thing, when you're a sample-based producer that goes out and digs for beats, the most important thing is storage. How to store your joints, man. A lot of dudes, they can't manage their record collection. That was one thing that my father taught me early. He was like, "Yo, you're getting a lot of records, man. You gotta know how to store them and make them easy to manage around." I started off with my joints alphabetized. That's how [producer] Paul C. had his records—alphabetized with the Levo sleeves and the plastic. Paul's shit was in pristine condition. He taught me that with the records, and my joints are in the same condition. Those are the tools, man, so I treat them right. Keep that dust down and shit. Paul C. . . . even before he would sample the shit, he used to pull it out, throw it on the platter . . . clean it all, sit there and carefully drop the needle on it and all that shit! That shit would come out sounding fresh, like boom![11]

Turntables and Mixers

The hip-hop DJ is an integral part of hip-hop music, with DJs such as Kool Herc and Grandmaster Flash providing the template that the music is built on (see p. 133-136). The DJ's instruments include the turntable and mixer, allowing them to play and manipulate records. The turntables are the record players that play the records, while the mixer is a piece of equipment that allows the sounds from the turntables to be mixed together and altered.

Grandwizard Theodore

The DJ sets the tone for the party. He has the records, the speakers, the amps—he has everything. The b-boy couldn't come out and break[dance] until the DJ was playing the music. And the rapper: all he has to do is show up and pick up the mic and just start rapping, but not until after the DJ had set everything up. Back in the day with some-one like Kool Herc, he was the DJ and he had rappers with him but he was the one out front and they just backed him up.[12]

Many beatmakers began as DJs and attribute being good at DJing to their success as beatmakers, as DJing usually leads to a large appreciation and knowledge of records. Manipulating sounds on a turntable also feeds into and overlaps with the skills needed to create tracks as a beatmaker.

DJ Premier

I do everything with a DJ mentality. DJing is my number one love. Producing is not my favorite thing, it's for paying my bills. Although, when I produce, I don't want any half-assed quality coming out. It has to sound great and I make sure that I put my all into it. Everything I do comes from DJing, because using samples is one of the ways in which we create music in the hip-hop world.[13]

Dr. Dre

I would definitely not be as good of a producer if I hadn't started DJing. Because that's where I really started paying attention to how records are made. I would critique and just listen and say, "I would have done this different." So that definitely was a stepping stone to what I'm doing now.[14]

DJ Revolution

I think it has a contributing factor when you get down to
the studio experience and actually making the music. I
definitely think that when you're a DJ and you have that
DJ edge and you bring that into the studio, it makes your
music better. It's like the difference between hiring a session musician to play the trumpet on your track and hiring an actual composer as well as a musician, somebody
who knows how to write the music, knows what sounds
good, someone who has a whole lot of experience. And I
think that if you weren't a DJ, that doesn't mean that
you're not going to be a great producer, but it just means
that you would bring an edge if you were a DJ beforehand.
I think what really makes the difference is in the perception of what a DJ does and is in hip-hop.[15]

As rappers and beatmakers became more popular, the DJ was often sidelined to just a supporting role, doing a few scratches on
hip-hop tracks and/or playing the instrumental tracks for rappers
to rap over at live shows, rather than being the main event. In
some cases this leads to DJs branching out on their own to make
records and hold events that further develop the craft of DJing,
where the focus is on scratching and mixing records in elaborate
ways.

DJ Revolution

Producers and MCs kinda just shut the door on the DJ;
[they] shut him out of the videos, shut him out of actually
having a feature on the song, shut him out of getting a shout-
out on the record and saying "yo, check my DJ out" . . . And
then when DJs felt like they weren't getting incorporated,
they kind of splintered off into their own little subculture,

and that's when "turntablism" was born, which was strictly about scratching and doing all this other stuff.[16]

Grandwizard Theodore

As time went by the rappers started phasing out the DJ as they, [the rappers,] became more and more popular and moved to the front. So I think it is great that the DJ is now making a comeback, 'cause the DJ played a major, major part in this hip-hop culture.[17]

While many different brands and models of turntables have been used over the years, one particular make has become a standard for hip-hop DJs: the Technics 1200, known for its reliability and sturdy build.

Pete Rock

You know how you need two arms and two legs? You need the 1200s. Those are a necessity right now. Hip-hop can't happen without those turntables. Doing a party can't happen without those turntables. They got new ones that try to look like the 1200s and feel like the 1200s and maybe even scratch like the 1200s, but those Technics are historical! This is a historical invention.[18]

Drum Machines

The term *drum machine* is usually used to refer to a machine which comes with prerecorded drum sounds that can then be programmed in different sequences, creating different rhythms. They differ from later sampling/sequencing machines as you cannot record in any sounds you like, you simply use the sounds which come with the machine.

One of the most widely used drum machines in hip-hop is the Roland TR-808 drum machine, often referred to simply as the "808." Its drum sounds were not considered realistic, but this became part of the machine's strength: it has unique and instantly recognizable hand claps, cowbells, and bass kicks, among other sounds.

Artists such as Kurtis Mantronik (see p. 96) used the 808 as the main source for the drums on a lot of songs—the 808 sounds on these records were then often sampled by later hip-hop artists, rather than directly from the machine itself.

Kurtis Mantronik

I had never heard anything like [Afrika] Bambaataa's "Planet Rock." He used the TR-808. My idea was to use the 808 at a much slower tempo to make it sound really big and boomy. "Fresh Is the Word" is really the sound of the TR-808. I liked its crispness, the fatness of the kick [drum sound], and because it was slower it had more of a guttural feeling. I didn't hear anybody use the 808 like that then, keeping it raw to its intended form, putting a loop on it and slowing it down. "Planet Rock" had all kinds of production tricks, but "Fresh Is the Word" was all 808. I didn't think I was doing anything new or different, it just felt good to me.[19]

Schoolly D

[On the song "Dis Groove Is Bad" is] when I first started fucking around with the 808, with the heavy, sub-low kick drum. . . . That was the first track that I used the 808 and the [E-mu] SP-12 on. I was sampling all those 808s off of old Mantronix records before that.[20]

Other artists have regularly used drum machine sounds to complement and enhance tracks that are otherwise entirely made from samples—in particular, they would often use the 808's bass kick drum sound to beef up the bottom end of the music.

Big Daddy Kane
Marley [Marl] had a gritty feel for music. Regardless of how clean or brand-new the record was that he was sampling, or how light the production may have been, he always gave it a really gritty feel when he sampled it. He always put the 808 to it and gave it a heavy bottom and warm feel.[21]

Rakim
Our engineer Patrick Adams did a lot of that . . . I'd basically just take my break beats and ideas in, and he'd sample it up and put the [Roland TR-]808 on it. Patrick was the guy who first turned me on to the 808. We'd dress up the beats.[22]

Q-Tip, A Tribe Called Quest
[On the song "Excursions,"] I put a reverse [Roland TR-]808 behind it, right before the beat actually kicks in.[23]

Samplers/Sequencers

One of the main types of beatmaking equipment, often the central piece in most beatmakers' set-ups, is a sampler and sequencer. This is a machine which both "samples" sounds by recording them in from records, TV, or any other audio input (rather than using prerecorded sounds that come with the machine), and is then also used to "sequence" those sounds, usually through tapping out rhythms by hand on a series of "pads," where each pad plays back a sampled sound. Two of the most popular and widely used sampler/sequencers are the E-mu SP-1200 and the Akai MPC.

E-mu SP-1200

The SP-1200, manufactured by E-mu and brought out in 1987, is responsible for a lot of the beats produced during hip-hop's golden age (see p. 147). It is an upgrade of the SP-12 which came out in 1986 and was also popular with beatmakers—the SP-1200 has more sampling time than its predecessor, so it can store more and longer sounds.

Buckwild
[The SP-1200] was such an amazing machine that [you] could do so much with. Some of the features on there made it the ultimate drum tool. Hip-hop was always a drum driven form of music. Whatever drums you would chop, coming out of the 1200 they would sound so raw. One of my favorite tracks was ["They Reminisce Over You (T.R.O.Y.)"], by Pete Rock [& C.L. Smooth]. Hearing the way those drums were chopped and the way they played it just sounds so crazy. The song mode, patterns, features . . . it has to be the most incredible machine, or the foundation of hip-hop. You could talk about the [drum machines like the] 808s or the 909s, but you know, our team, we used the 1200 more as our foundation than anything else. There was so much that you could do that it's not funny.[24]

Pete Rock
Everything that you ever heard from me back in the day was the SP-1200. That machine made "Reminisce" ["They

Reminisce Over You (T.R.O.Y.)"], "Straighten It Out," "Shut 'Em Down [Remix]," "Jump Around [Remix]."[25]

Even though it was state of the art and one of the most advanced machines at the time, the SP-1200 had a low amount of sampling time compared to today's equipment (i.e., the number of seconds of sound that could be recorded into the machine was relatively limited). This meant producers had to be creative with what they sampled and how they used the samples, as they could not simply loop long segments of another record.

DJ Clark Kent
Back in the day, when I had the [SP]-1200, you had 10 seconds! You could never put 10 seconds on one pad. Each pad had the ability to take 2.5 seconds. And if you took 2.5 seconds on one pad at one time, the next pad wouldn't let you take a whole 2.5 seconds. It would give you like a second or 1.2 seconds. So you had to become creative. Being an arranger . . . you had no choice![26]

DJ Muggs, Cypress Hill
I didn't have a lot of records [when I began beatmaking]. I had a couple crates of records. The first time, there might be nothing on those records. But I'd keep going through them, and find the littlest pieces. I had the SP-1200, so all we had was ten seconds of sampling time . . . it was just all these little sounds. Whatever you have, you're going to adapt to it. So I just adapted to what I had.[27]

Hank Shocklee, the Bomb Squad
There's little tricks that were developed on it. For example, you got [a limited number of] seconds of sample time to divide amongst eight pads. So depending on how much

you use on each pad, you decrease the amount of sample time that you have. [So] you take a 33 ⅓ record and play it on 45, and you cheat the system [by sampling the sounds in faster so they take up less room, then slowing them back down using one of the machine's functions]. [Another] aspect that we created is out of a mistake—one day I was playing "Black Steel in the Hour of Chaos" and it came out real muffled. I couldn't hear any of the high-end part of it. I found out that if you put the phono or quarter-inch jack halfway in, it filters the high frequency. Now I just got the bass part of the sample. I was like, "Oh, shit, this is the craziest thing on the planet!"[28]

Buckwild

With the 1200, the drums were always so hard because of the 12 bit sampler [which recorded sounds in lower, grittier quality]. There were certain things I wish I could take with it and put that into today's samplers, because it's missing. There were less options but it made you work. Your limitations make your brain think more.[29]

Akai MPC

In 1988 Akai launched what was to become the main successor to E-mu's SP-1200—the MPC (originally MIDI Production Center, now Music Production Controller). It allowed more sampling time than the SP-1200 and had a pad layout that a lot of beatmakers prefer.

Pete Rock

I used the MPC on *Soul Survivor II*. That was kind of the beginning of using it. I thought it had a thinner sound than the SP, but it had way more sample time—like three minutes. So, can't beat that. I got hundreds of beats on the SP-1200, but I like the MPC. I'm really starting to get in the midst of it now.[30]

Alchemist

I think it's probably hands down the most handy machine when it comes to production. It has just what you need. It pretty much defined the standard of production for beats. I feel like with the MPC it's the standard. Partly because of the swing capabilities, [MPC Swing] in it, which made the drums for a lot of producers over the years [because it adds a less rigid and more "swung" feel to the rhythm of the drums]. You knew automatically because of their drum swing that it was something the MPC did. Once I got to the MPC, I was like, "YES, this is what I was trying to do the whole time!" I can't think of any machine that's similar . . . [other machines after the MPC] always seem like they have to have the 16 pads [as their layout] and basically simulate the style of the MPC. I was watching a demo of [a newer machine] and thought, "this is very MPC-esque."[31]

There are various models of the MPC and several of these continue to be manufactured, making it easier to obtain than the SP-1200, which ceased production in the late 1990s. Different beatmakers prefer different models of MPC—generally later models have more sampling time and more features.

DJ Premier

The engineer I was using in the early 1990s introduced me to the MPC60 and he was like, "Hey, you should try this—the way you lay tracks down and adjust levels, it's kind of like a tape recorder without the tape." I gave it a try and have been addicted to it ever since. Akai gave me an MPC2500, but I have not yet used it, because it's a learning curve, and I have to learn all the commands. I like the difficulties of the older equipment.[32]

Dr. Dre

I love using the MPC3000. I like setting up like four or five different MPC3000s, so I don't have to keep changing disks. So I have them all lined up, and I have different drum sounds in each one, and then we use one for sequencing the keyboard.[33]

Some producers don't actually sample sounds directly into the MPC, they use a separate sampler to store the sounds (a machine that can only sample sounds and does not let you sequence those sounds) and they use the MPC just as a sequencer in order to "trigger" the sounds from the separate sampler in different rhythms.

DJ Premier

I don't sample with the MPC60, I just use it to trigger drums. Instead I sample in the [Akai] S950 and trigger them from the MPC—everything, also my keyboards, is [connected] to the MPC.[34]

The MPC remains the standard beatmaking machine today, despite legions of imitators, including computer software that mimics the MPC's functions.

Alchemist

In general, MPC always has and always will be the standard as far as when you're talking about rap, beats, and production. You know, my favorite producers from day one were Premier—MPC. Pete Rock? MPC. Diamond D? MPC. I mean I could go down the list forever. It's pretty much the standard. It's good to be able to even follow in those footsteps and keep that tradition going forward. You know, making music that comes out of that machine, it sounds crazy. Impersonation has gotten to extreme levels with regards to MPC with people trying to copy it, but I think at the end of the day with the sound that comes out of it, I can usually call it. I can say, "that's [an] MPC, yo."[35]

Keyboards

Lots of different makes and models of keyboard have been used in the creation of hip-hop music throughout its history and they have been used in various ways. Earlier hip-hop records would sometimes use keyboards as the primary instrument, with melodies and rhythms being performed live, because without samplers and sequencers, the parts could not simply be recorded once and looped easily.

Arthur Baker
[Afrika] Bambaataa wanted to use the keyboardist who had played on a record that he liked, and this turned out to be John Robie . . . John played everything by hand, nothing was sequenced on [Afrika Bambaataa's record,] "Planet Rock"—we didn't have a sequencer at that time.[36]

Often, beatmakers will use keyboards alongside samples, and sometimes keyboards are used to replay samples, if a beatmaker does not want to use an actual segment of a record.

Dr. Dre

I love the old school [keyboard] sounds, ARP String Ensemble, Rhodes, old school Clavinet, the whole shit. I'm a big keyboard fan.[37]

Some beatmakers collect keyboards to add to the range of sounds that they can use on their records—these range from older, classic keyboards to more cutting-edge, modern keyboards.

RZA, Wu-Tang Clan

On [GZA's] *Liquid Swords* album—all the synth you hear is the Nord Lead, which was made by Clavia. I have more than thirty keyboards—but I'm not sure if I have a true favorite. I like the Fantom, but I don't have a main keyboard. Still, I have to give a lot of respect to the Kurzwell. The ASR-10 is my favorite keyboard in history, but the Kurzwell would be my second favorite. Also, the Kurzwell can actually read the ASR-10 disc. So when I did [the album] *Wu-Tang Forever*, I took all my ASR and EPS discs and just stuck them into the Kurzwell. It's compatible like that, so it's like the overfiend of the whole shit. At first, I was interested in more chopping sounds, then I got more into keyboards.[38]

PART III

7. Old School / New School

The Old School (1973-1984)

The *old school* runs from the creation of hip-hop music in 1973, up until the *new school* started to emerge and dominate around 1984. The old school is hip-hop's first major era and includes many innovations and foundational techniques that remain with the genre today.

Breaks

Hip-hop music's core, the musical element which spawned the whole genre, is the "break." This is often found in funk or soul music, but it can be from any genre—it is where the band "breaks" down the music during a song to just the drums, percussion, and sometimes a minimal bass line or other rhythmic element. Kool Herc is the DJ widely regarded as "inventing" hip-hop music in the early 1970s by focusing on breaks—playing just this part of each record so that people could dance to the most rhythmically intense parts of various songs.

Grandmaster Flash

[Kool Herc] wasn't playing the whole song. He jumped right to the middle of the song; the part where the rhythm section gets down to the basics of business. He would pick up the needle and drop it down on the vinyl. Pick it up and drop it down. Drums. A little bass. That's it. That's the break. Fuck the melody, forget the chorus, and leave the verses alone; we're talking about the pure rhythmic groove.[1]

Breaks can be found across almost all genres of music that use drums: jazz, rock, salsa, soul, funk, R&B, and heavy metal, among others. Afrika Bambaataa was one of the key early figures who helped to introduce a wide range of genres for hip-hop to draw breaks and influences from.

DJ Breakout

Bambaataa used to play the wildest records in the whole entire world. He played stuff like Bugs Bunny—it's got a beat on it. Everybody was breakdancing to that.[2]

Afrika Bambaataa

I'd throw on [the Beatles'] *Sgt Pepper's Lonely Hearts Club Band*—just that drum part. One, two, three, BAM—and they'd be screaming and partying. I'd throw on the Monkees, "Mary, Mary, where are you going?"—and they'd start going crazy. I'd say, "You just danced to the Monkees." They'd say, "You liar. I didn't dance to no Monkees." I'd like to catch people who categorize records.[3]

While Kool Herc and Afrika Bambaataa provided the template that hip-hop music is based on, it was the more precise technical skills of DJs such as Grandmaster Flash and Grandwizard Theodore that led to further creative expansion and development of hip-hop music in the mid-1970s. Although these early figures were DJs at parties (rather than beatmakers who made music that would be released on records), their innovations with breaks provided the basis that would later be used when hip-hop transitioned from parties onto records in 1979.

Grandmaster Flash developed intricate methods for extending a break so that it sounded like the beat never stopped playing. He did this by creating techniques where two copies of the same record could be cued up and played directly after each other, essentially "looping" the break manually with two turntables, so that it played over and over again, seamlessly.

Grandmaster Flash

As monumental as Herc's insight was, there was something that bothered me about his style. He didn't care about keeping the actual beat locked in tight; he didn't make the switch from one song to the next in a clean cut that matched the beats, bars, and phrases of the two jams. He just mashed one song on top of the other.[4] Using two copies of the same record—one to play and one to cue up while the other was playing—was the easy part. That was the thing that Herc had already figured out. That's what made him so popular. The hard part—the part Herc *hadn't* figured out—was playing them right on time.[5] My electronic knowledge had to come into play. I had to create what I called a "peek-a-boo" system. It allowed me to pre-hear the music in my ear before I pushed it out to the people . . . I used to play the break with what's called a backspin or the "clock theory" [reading the label of the record to spin it backward to the place where the selected segment began]. Now I was able to play the break of all these songs in succession, back to back to back to back to back.[6]

Grandwizard Theodore is noted for inventing the "scratch," where a record is moved back and forth against the needle, creating a "scratching" noise. This allows rhythmic patterns to be created while playing breaks and other sounds from records.

Grandwizard Theodore

Back in the days, Grandmaster Flash invented this way of rubbing a record, but he usually just rubbed it once and just let it go. What I did was give it a rhythm; I made a tune out of it, rubbing it for three, four minutes, making it a scratch. Before that, a DJ would have his earphones on, and I could see him moving the record back and forth, but the people couldn't hear him moving it back and forth. What I did was, I just switched it over so the people could hear the record going back and forth, and it made a beat out of it.[7]

Party Rhymes

Early rapping came from announcements over the microphone at parties, which led to crowd-motivating chants, eventually evolving into simple "party rhymes," where the emphasis was on encouraging people to dance and have a good time, as well as braggadocio used to highlight the skill and prominence of the DJ and MC (this is detailed further on p. 54–56).

Kurtis Blow

[The earliest hip-hop MCs]—these guys were just announcers. The next level was the crowd response . . . [where MCs] had routines . . . and [they] did it with a little rhythm you know: "Throw your hands in the air, everybody now, we don't need no music, come on y'all say it, so just clap your hands everybody, and everybody body clap your hands! If you're not too skinny or not too fat, everybody say and you know that!"[8]

These fun party rhymes were a main feature of old-school hip-hop, both at actual parties, and also when hip-hop began appearing on commercially released records in 1979.

Prodigy, Mobb Deep

The Sugar Hill Gang, the Cold Crush [Brothers] and all that. It was fun. It wasn't really about being too lyrical. You're really not saying nothing. And that's how rap started. So that's the essence of it. It's just fun and just making your money and getting popular and repping your crew and where you're [from] and all of that.[9]

Kool G Rap

[At first I was] just watching the older dudes do it in the park . . . I saw dudes on the microphone just really keeping the party amped and charged up—just being masters of ceremony, where the word *MC* comes from, just keeping the party alive.[10]

From DJs to Live Bands on Record

Originally, the music that was rapped over was provided by a DJ playing breaks at parties. However, when hip-hop moved into the studio to be recorded, it was mainly played by in-house studio bands. Rather than having a DJ extend the break from a vinyl record, session musicians would replay the breaks from popular records.

Sha-Rock

When we'd perform live, our DJs was a part of our show, doing the mixes, the introductions, the records. But when we went into the studio . . . we used a live band; we didn't use a DJ. . . . We never really used the DJs in the studio; we always used live bands.[11]

A lot of the image and the sound was also based on popular funk and disco music of the time. Old-school hip-hop artists would often rerecord the instrumentals of disco hits to rap over, such as Chic's "Good Times," famously used on Sugarhill Gang's 1979 single, "Rapper's Delight," one of the first commercially released hip-hop records.

Keith Leblanc

I was brought up with James Brown, Muscle Shoals, Parliament/Funkadelic, Gap Band, and Cameo, so playing the rap stuff [as a drummer in Sugarhill Records' studio band] wasn't much of a stretch from what we were already doing.[12]

Elaborate Image

Also central to the old school's style was the image and outfits. The image that most of the groups and artists presented was far removed from what it would later become—old-school performers would often wear elaborate outfits associated with funk and disco, in stark contrast to the more street-oriented look of the new-school artists.

Sal Abbatiello

The whole scene was leather and fringes and sparkly and rhinestones . . . made outfits.[13]

Grandmaster Caz

[We were doing] shows in leather outfits with fur shit hanging off of us . . . the cats who came after us . . . they're like, "Look, we're going back, we're going to put on the sneakers, the jeans. We're going to look just like we look when we're at a party."[14]

Rakim

Coming from the hood, they wanted to be stars. They had the leather on, the chains on, they made it look bigger than it was. [R&B/funk singer] Rick James was killing them back then. Rick James kept a leather suit on. So at that time, I guess to look like a star it was leather. Melle Mel and [Kool] Moe Dee . . . if you remember Moe Dee, he had the leather suits on, [it] made rappers look like stars.[15]

Importance of the Term
Old School

Many people misuse the term *old school* in a hip-hop music context, as they assume it means any hip-hop music that isn't recent. Referring to music from the new school and the golden age of hip-hop as *old school* is as incorrect as referring to heavy metal artists as indie rock or psychedelic-jazz artists as bebop.

Many hip-hop artists take exception to this misuse of the term, suggesting that it shows a lack of respect for hip-hop's history and its different eras, and it encourages people to simply group all the "older" music together without realizing its significance.

Melle Mel
It's a smack in the face to even call [Run-D.M.C. and Notorious BIG] old school. They just throw Run-[D.M.C.] and them in there with us, then they just label it all old school. Even Rakim and Big Daddy Kane. It's not fair to them or us. If it's old they just lump it all together. The original old school is cats like [Grandmaster Flash and the] Furious 5, Herculords and [Afrika] Bam[Baataa] and the Zulus . . . Cold Crush, Fantastic 5, Busy Bee, Funky 4, Spoonie Gee, Treacherous 3, Kurtis Blow, Luv Bug Starski, Fearless 4, and a couple other groups.[16]

Ced Gee, Ultramagnetic MCs
Don't call groups like us and KRS[-One] "old school," because we're not. "Old school" is [Afrika] Bambaataa, Kool Herc, and Grandmaster Flash. See, when you call us "old school," you're losing history and culture. We learned from those guys and propelled it to the next level.[17]

Hip-hop artists encourage fans to listen to and learn about hip-hop's eras, as it is important for the preservation of its history. Being familiar with its time line allows for a greater understanding of hip-hop.

T3, Slum Village
Right now I think MCs should do the history, go back. Learn about some of these original rappers. The only reason why I say that, is not saying it to be like school, but

[fans] need to respect rap a little more . . . listen to some of the old school and listen to a bit of the new school.[18]

The New School (1984 onwards)

The new school era marks the shift away from the lighthearted party rhymes and funk/disco style of the old school into a harsher, rawer sound and look. Starting with the emergence of Run-D.M.C. (consisting of rappers Run and D.M.C. alongside DJ Jam Master Jay) with their 1983 single "It's Like That/Sucker M.C.'s," the new-school sound had become the more popular style by 1984, with releases by LL Cool J and the Beastie Boys in a similar vein, as well as Run-D.M.C.'s full debut album.

Bill Adler

[Run-D.M.C.'s] impact has been nothing less than revolutionary. Although they debuted three-and-a-half years after Sugarhill Records and the Sugarhill Gang launched rap as a serious musical force, Run-D.M.C. were the first to embody, without apology, the music, poetry, fashion, body language, and worldview of New York's black male teens— the hip-hop culture that had been brewing underground for ten years when "It's Like That/Sucker M.C.'s" dropped like a bomb in the spring of 1983.[19]

Grandmaster Caz

Run-D.M.C. was the cutoff point between us and hip-hop after that. That was the end of the era for Grandmaster Flash and the Furious 5, for the Cold Crush [Brothers], for the Funky 4+1, for the Fearless 4s and for the Fantastic 5s and all that. That was the end of our era, when Run-D.M.C. and them came into the game.[20]

A Harder Sound

The style of the music changed dramatically during the shift from old school to new school—while old-school records were based mostly around in-house studio bands replaying more lightweight hits, the new school brought in abrasive drum machine sounds, often accented with loud guitar noises.

Russell Simmons

At that time it was most important to us to do shit that was very simple and real. Our whole thing was let's try to be real and the realest thing that you could do was just put a drumbeat with nothing but a drumbeat—so a record like [Run--D.M.C.'s] "Sucker M.C.'s." And also . . . loud. So we wanted guitars, because we would always scratch guitars, but not scratch guitar *riffs*, just the noise: rrrruuhhhunn! That whole [thing where] you cut the beat and you give it dynamics.[21]

Bill Adler

One day after school, Run and [D.M.C.] took all their rhymes over to [producer] Larry [Smith]'s place in South Jamaica [in New York]. Larry and Russ[ell Simmons] were up in the attic, where Larry had a little recording studio—and where he'd devised a radically new arrangement for a rap record. . . . [Larry] had created a track that left plenty of room for vocals, featuring little more than a drum machine smashing out a stark beat, dressed up just a bit with the occasional synthesizer swoosh and sting.[22]

Keith Leblanc

When the drum machine first came out, I saw my job opportunities [as a drummer] flying out of the window. Now anybody could make a rap record in their bedroom. But then it dawned on me that I could program a drum machine better than any engineer.[23]

The new sound was heavily pushed by Russell Simmons's Def Jam record label, which made the earlier labels, such as the previously dominant Sugarhill Records, sound tame and unfashionable in the process.

Reggie Reg
When Def Jam came out, that was like the nail in Sugarhill's coffin. Sugarhill had [most of the best acts], everybody. But they wouldn't change. Def Jam was a newer, fresher label. They weren't doing the old stuff that Sugarhill was doing. . . . We used to plead with them, "Yo, we need a drum machine. Forget about that live drum player you got there; we need a 808 [drum machine]. We need to make it electronic." And they just didn't want to change.[24]

A "Realer" Image

The look of hip-hop artists and groups moved from the excesses of the disco outfits to a more hard-core, street image that complemented the new sound. The change in look made the contrast between the music of the old and new schools even clearer and made it harder for the old-school style to survive.

Run, Run-D.M.C.
We used to come to our gigs dressed in jeans, ready to tear shit up. And the Fearless Four always had these leather suits on and white boots and their hair braided. They said,

"Man, y'all come just like y'all come off the street!" I said, "That's how we coming, boyee. That's how we living!"[25]

Jam Master Jay, Run-D.M.C.

When people seen us, they seen that we was regular normal people who didn't go around with no braids in our hair, flicking them around. People tend to like what's real. And we was real.[26]

Melle Mel, Grandmaster Flash and the Furious Five

What Run and them did . . . it was very simple, they dressed like and had the same image as their fans. Then every group that was big that came after them was a little grimier till you have what's going on right now. Our fans couldn't be us. We had $1,500 tailor made leather suits. We shopped all over the world. The best they could hope to be was a scaled down version of us and it would look corny. So when Run and them started dressing like the dudes on the corners of Hollis, Queens [in New York], street cred started to mean more than creativity. With us, once you were stars you were bigger than the streets. It counteracted what we did, where we set it up to be big superstars. That threw everything out of whack, because now people think the streets have something to offer.[27]

DMC, Run-D.M.C.

I was so disappointed—these ain't the guys I was always worshipping! They came out dressed in their braids and shit. Corny! I thought, "Don't you know? You're Grandmaster Flash, you knucklehead! You're supposed to be him! What are you doing dressing like this and disappointing me?" But that just gave me the confidence to think, "Fuck it! Me and [Run] and Jay are gonna set an example!"[28]

Rakim

After the leather era, it was jackets and hats. Run and them came out with the hats, so we were kinda looking for something [like that too]. So [it meant we had to] look not just like Hollywood stars, but urban stars. Stars from the hood.[29]

Bill Adler

Run-D.M.C.'s dedication to [the more hard-core] b-boy style had earned them a salute from *Details* magazine as one of the handful of Most Important Fashion Influences of the Eighties.[30]

The New School and the Golden Age

The new school has never really formally ended or been abruptly superseded—however, because the term *new school* is mostly used to signal the end of the old school, then the further away from 1984 you get, the less useful the term is and the less it is used.

Very soon after the shift into the new-school sound in 1984, hip-hop entered a period of intense innovation and development, known as *the golden age*, starting in 1986 and ending around 1994. Groups and artists from this period are most commonly described as being from the golden age, and this is the dominant term for that period of time. However, golden age artists are still sometimes referred to as *new school*, especially if they are from the early part of the golden age.

RZA, Wu-Tang Clan

GZA [of the Wu-Tang Clan] and myself were the babies of the old school guys—from Force MDs, to Cold Crush Brothers, to the Furious Five, Grandmaster Flash, the Fantastic Five, the Disco Four Plus One More, the Funky Four Plus One More. At the time we were coming up, the *new school* brothers were Rakim, KRS-One, Big Daddy Kane, Biz Markie, Marley Marl, the whole Juice Crew team, as well as brothers like Just-Ice and other MCs that didn't make it. We were absorbing all of it back then, we were the ones being nurtured by them.[31]

TR Love, Ultramagnetic MCs

We came in with [the record] "Ego Trippin'" and things started blowing up from there. . . . This was around the beginnings of the *new school*. Us, [MC] Shan, Eric B. and Rakim. . . . [32]

8. The Golden Age of Hip-Hop

One of the most important time periods (arguably *the* most important) in hip-hop music's history is what's known as hip-hop's *golden age*, also sometimes alternatively referred to as the golden "era."

Oxford Dictionary
Golden age: the period when a specified art or activity is at its peak.[1]

This is the era widely agreed on by hip-hop artists, fans, scholars, and critics to be the most innovative, creative, and influential period in hip-hop music's history. While there is also incredible music made before and after the golden age, many of the biggest leaps forward were made during this era, and many of the most acclaimed albums and artists came out at this time. Hip-hop's core techniques went from being relatively simple to being fully developed by the end of the period.

Time Period (1986–1994)

Although the suggested beginning and end points sometimes vary slightly, the golden age of hip-hop is generally thought to have started in 1986 and ended around 1994. The starting point is less disputed than the end point: it begins around 1986 when tracks such as Eric B. & Rakim's "My Melody" revolutionized rapping, big advancements were being made in beatmaking, and Run-D.M.C.'s incredibly successful third album, *Raising Hell*, made hip-hop music more visible. The end point is sometimes said to be as early as 1992 or as late as 1996.

Young MC

A lot of us older guys can point to 1986 through 1993 as the "golden era." Maybe you can squeeze that down a little bit, but in there, if you're starting with Run [DMC's third album] and going all the way through to [Dr.] Dre and Snoop [Dogg], is what would essentially be considered the golden era.[2]

MC Serch

I think that the MCs from let's say '86 to '94–'95, in that ten-year time frame, were probably the most talented MCs to ever come out of hip-hop, I don't think there has been anyone that has been any better in this generation in terms of wordplay, in terms of cadence, in terms of flow, in terms of enunciation, in terms of just pure charisma on a track than those nine or ten years of hip-hop.[3]

Phife, A Tribe Called Quest

KRS[-One] or Big Daddy Kane and stuff like that—that was the golden era of hip-hop to me, when those guys were coming out and doing their own thing. You know, LL [Cool J] had his thing, Rakim had his, KRS[-One] had his, Biz Markie had his, everybody was holding their own.[4]

Brother Ali

In the late '80s, when people like KRS-One and Chuck D came out, and Rakim, I started writing . . . I was really inspired by the jump that the art of writing rhymes took in the late '80s and early '90s and that's when I started writing myself.[5]

Innovation

Innovation was an essential component of the golden age, which explains why the era is so respected and influential. It was a time of unbridled innovation, where the craft was developed and updated literally from month to month.

This was fostered and encouraged by a belief, almost a "rule," throughout the genre that you had to bring something new to the table. Copying someone else's style or doing something that someone else had already done was heavily discouraged—the person would be called a "biter" and was said to be "biting" someone else's style.

Zumbi, Zion I

I think back in the day, the idea behind why you MCed might have been a little different—it was much more about being original and having style. Whereas nowadays there's definitely a lot of clones that get accepted as fresh artists that I think back in the day would definitely have been biters.[6]

Fredro Starr, Onyx

Rule number one—don't bite. That's rule number one in rap, don't bite . . . you gotta have originality. You gotta bring something new to the game and stay original, just do what you feel like doing.[7]

T3, Slum Village

Basically what I'm saying is, okay, I want to be a hip-hop guy, I wanna bring something new to the game . . . So I gotta come with my aspect and get my inspiration from elsewhere and that way I can bring my new aspect to this game. So I won't say the same thing they said or did, or come across the same way they came across.[8]

Innovation in Content

Content in hip-hop lyrics went from rapping mostly about partying and braggadocio, and the occasional socially conscious track, to vastly expanding into a huge array of different topics and themes.

Prodigy, Mobb Deep

As rap progressed, people got more serious about the lyrics . . . you've got different levels of it. You've got the conscious rap, you've got the hardcore rap, you've got the party songs, you've got the strip club songs, you've got the different types of things. And that just shows the progression of this, it's not just one thing.[9]

Among the different topics and styles of content introduced and developed during the golden age were: political themes, violence, "Horrorcore" and shock-value content, postmodern pop culture references, Mafioso and Mafia-inspired content, humor and satire, abstract content, stories, kung fu and martial arts, relationships and sex, selling and using drugs, philosophy and science, religion, street life, and socially conscious content. Alongside this expansion were developments in the usage of many literary and poetic techniques such as analogies, similes, metaphors, and punchlines.

This level of development in content during the golden age presented a problem for those who came after it: so many topics had already been covered at such a high level that it was harder to innovate and to find subjects that had not yet been tackled.

Innovation in Flow

Flow is the term used to describe the rhyme and rhythm techniques used in rapping. Both underwent drastic developments and increased complexity from the beginning to the end of the golden age.

Rhymes went from simple "cool/rule/fool/school" rhymes (as in Run-D.M.C.'s "King of Rock" 1985), to compound rhymes, where multiple syllables rhyme with each other, such as "pig a day habit" and "ricochet rabbit" (from Kool G Rap & DJ Polo's "Letters" 1992). Additionally, more rhymes were often packed into each bar of music, resulting in raps with long runs of rhymes.

Brother J, X Clan
When [Big Daddy] Kane came out, everybody was, "*going* and *showing* and *flowing*" and so on, and doing all that [continuous rhyming].[10]

As with content, once bars of music were filled entirely with rhyming words, and rhyme schemes had grown ever more complex, there was little room for further extensive innovation. Most of the rhyming techniques had reached their logical conclusion—they went from a few very simple rhymes in obvious places, to many complex rhymes in a variety of places.

During the same period, rhythm in rapping also expanded, going from simplistic, "sing-songy" rhythms, to intricate, varied percussive techniques. If you listen to LL Cool J's "Rock the Bells" from 1985 and then listen to Das EFX's "Mic Checka" from 1992 or Organized Konfusions's "Bring It On" from 1994, it will give a clear picture of the leaps made in rhythmic techniques over the course of the golden age.

Gift of Gab, Blackalicious

I'm a style junkie, so I was always into new styles. I always liked hearing albums like [De La Soul's] *3 Feet High and Rising* or Freestyle Fellowship's *Innercity Griots*, or Public Enemy's *It Takes a Nation of Millions.* . . . . It helped me to grow as an artist to hear artists like KRS-One and Kool Keith who were really flipping styles, because I was really into styles—I was really into, "Wow, I've never heard anybody rap like that before."[11]

T3, Slum Village

My background is more on the [rhythmic] style, [rather than focused on content], so I was more into certain albums. Back in the '90s, there was a lot of rappers [doing a lot of different rhythms], like the Rumpletilskinz did a lot of lyrical styles, and Leaders of the New School. Back then they did a lot of [flow] techniques that inspired me and my whole style.[12]

Innovation in Production

Production evolved in two major ways—innovation in the core techniques of constructing the music and also in the types of genres and sounds that were used to make hip-hop music. As with rapping, the level of innovation and competition made it vital that each new release pushed the boundaries in order to stay relevant.

Mike D, Beastie Boys

Our first album, [*Licensed To Ill*], was just a collection of songs, really—it didn't really work together as an album . . . but I remember, at different points of making and finishing *Paul's Boutique*, listening to [Public Enemy's album] *Nation of Millions* and [De La Soul's album] *3 Feet High and Rising* and feeling both excited and depressed. I was excited because both were incredibly great records, but depressed because whatever we made wouldn't really mean anything, as they were so good.[13]

Important music-creation techniques that were introduced and/or developed during the golden age include: sampling individual sounds from records rather than looping a whole portion, layering sampled loops on top of each other, chopping up samples to further manipulate them into new patterns, filtering samples to remove certain elements such as the bass or the higher pitched instruments, programming drum machines and sequencers, and creating collages of many samples.

Afrika Bambaataa

You got all styles of hip-hop. . . . You got your hard beats, you got your gangsta rap, you got your electro-funk sound which came from the party rock sound, you got your Miami bass, you got the go-go from DC . . . Teddy Riley, he came to Bronx River parties and heard go-go music and just flipped it up and now you got "new jack swing." All of this was all part of hip-hop.[14]

Sources for sampling broadened to include an even wider range of genres than previously used, including: rock, heavy metal, funk, soul, R&B, jazz, blues, reggae/ragga, electronic music/dance, country, film dialogue, and film sound tracks. Big leaps were also made in developing instrumental hip-hop with no vocals, as well as techniques with keyboards and incorporating live instrumentation.

Matt Dike, Dust Brothers

I remember having this discussion with [Beastie Boys member Adam "MCA"] Yauch, and him saying, "Let's just go completely over the top and sample everything. Let's make this the nail in the coffin for sampling." And that's kind of what happened.[15]

Influence and Longevity

Music that is exceptionally innovative is also strongly influential—if someone has made large strides forward in the genre, then subsequent artists learn from them, incorporating their new methods to stay relevant and using the new techniques to improve their music. Many current acclaimed hip-hop artists point to the golden age as the source of both their inspiration and their initial instruction in how to create hip-hop music.

Tech N9ne

I studied all these [golden age] MCs, from KRS-One, to Rakim, to Public Enemy, to NWA, to Mantronix. . . .[16]

R.A. The Rugged Man

I always go back to the golden era with the [Big Daddy] Kanes and the Rakims and the Kool G Raps and all of that.[17]

Papoose

Like every other child in the ghetto I knew all the hottest records around . . . Big Daddy Kane, [Kool] G Rap, LL

[Cool J], Rakim, Slick Rick, the list goes on. Definitely, I knew all the hottest songs.[18]

MC Serch
I think everyone as a writer who came up in the '80s was influenced in some way, shape, or form by Rakim.[19]

As with all genres, the notable, innovative, groundbreaking, carefully crafted work stays relevant and is constantly referenced, while the more faddish and formulaic music, even if popular at the time, often fades from memory. Golden age hip-hop songs are still listened to regularly today and each new wave of hip-hop fans hears and learns about the classic artists and albums, keeping them continually relevant.

Young MC
A lot of the artists who can do shows are artists my age [from the golden age], as opposed to guys who came out with records around 2000 or 2001 . . . So me, 20 years after my hit, I can get shows where guys who came out a decade after me and sold more records than me can't.[20]

Pete Rock
That's always great [when I hear people say they love my classic records like "T.R.O.Y." from 1992]. To see that you were able to do a record that lasted for so long and touched so many people is great. I've never heard anything bad about that record ever since the day I made it, and that says a lot. To this day I'm still a DJ, so when I'm in the club DJing and play it people still go nuts. That goes to show you how much the golden era is effective, even right now.[21]

Diversity

The golden age is also known for its extreme diversity—a result of the willingness to innovate, experiment, and go in different directions. Artists prided themselves on having their own style and separating themselves from each other through diverse sounds, content, and images.

Pharoahe Monch

In the golden era of Chuck D, Kool G Rap, EPMD, Rakim, De La Soul, Big Daddy Kane, Kool Keith . . . you were dealing with a lot of choice and different styles of artists that were prospering, but not off the same trendiness. EPMD was way different from LL Cool J and Public Enemy. But now you get a clutter of artists on a label that all pretty much have a similar sound and work with the same producers and so on.[22]

Kool G Rap

The era I'm from, everybody strived to stand out and be their own person and to have their own character and have their own image. It's like you didn't wanna come out and be another Chuck D, you didn't wanna come out and be another KRS-One, you wanted to be as good as those rappers, but you wanted to be you though.[23]

During the golden age, hip-hop was able to present many different, and often conflicting, sounds and styles. Gangsta rappers such as N.W.A. and Spice 1 coexisted with groups from the other end of the spectrum, who touched on culture, politics, and positivity, such as X Clan and Arrested Development.

Myka 9, Freestyle Fellowship

[They] were putting messages in the music and coming with real lyrics, on through the '80s when you had Kool Moe Dee, Ultramagnetic MCs, the early days of LL Cool J, Rakim, KRS-One, where they were very, very technical, where they were talking about physics and talking about metaphysics and things like that. Then also at that same time you had the Pee-Wee Jam with Joe-Ski Love and you had a lot of silly songs that would come out, Fat Boys, stuff like that.[24]

The End of the Golden Age

While most fans, artists, and critics agree that there is still very worthwhile and interesting hip-hop music being made, they also generally agree that overall, the level of creativity dropped after the golden age—hence why it has an end point, whether it is as early as 1992 or as late as 1996.

CeeLo Green

I just felt like the bar was lowered. And this is not to insult anyone, it's just an observation. But I was born out of the golden era of MCing. I'm talking about the Brother Js from X Clan, and the KRS-Ones, and the Rakims.[25]

AZ

Back in the day it was more lyrical, more conceptual. Right now it's more partying and sing-along songs, but it's a different part of the game—can't be mad, I'm not mad at it at all, it is what it is—[but] back then you had to be a dart thrower to even be considered an MC. You had to have concepts.[26]

Vinnie Paz, Jedi Mind Tricks

[I prefer the hip-hop songs of] the mid to late '80s and early '90s, I think everything was better about them back then. I mean if you listen to records from Juice Crew, they're just incredible. All the stuff that I love [from then] I think is way more incredible than the stuff today.[27]

One reason for this is that so much was done during the golden age, that it left little room for further innovation. By around 1994, so much ground had been covered, so many new techniques had been introduced and developed, that it was difficult to make new discoveries, and any that were made were going to appear minor compared to the huge leaps forward of the golden age. Several other factors also contributed, compounding the problem.

Lack of Innovation and Experimentation

As the golden age was dependent on innovation, one of the things that ended it was a gradual *lack* of innovation. After 1994, a lot of hip-hop records became safer and more formulaic. While there are notable exceptions, the norm after the golden age was to be less adventurous.

Hank Shocklee, the Bomb Squad

The only thing that I see missing from today is the area of experimentation. We're not experimenting enough like we could be, like we did back in the days. The other thing is originality. We should all be striving to not sound like the next, but to sound different and apart from. Those are the only two areas that I miss from the golden age of hip-hop. I want to experiment, give [a group] their own voice, give them a sound that's separate and different from anything else that's out there right now. You don't have to conform to anything.[28]

Pigeon John

I think that in general there is less of an adventure nowadays, just less adventurous times, I think personally, someone needs to revive some spirit of adventure because it's hella boring . . . country is more adventurous than hip-hop nowadays, hip-hop isn't as adventurous as [R&B pop group] 3LW.[29]

Trying to Sound the Same, Instead of Different

The lack of innovation and experimentation immediately led to another problem: everything sounding similar instead of distinct, as more and more artists used tried-and-tested formulas instead of breaking the mold.

Chuck D, Public Enemy

I think today's MCs are more trying to figure out how to be similar and I think the older MCs always tried to figure out how to be different from each other.[30]

Kool G Rap

[Some newer artists] lack the drive to stand out amongst everybody else. I mean I'm not saying all of them, but on a mass level. Nowadays so many people are trying be the same like this guy, the same like that guy. When it's on a mass scale, when everybody's sounding the same, then that's when the music gets fucked up, because it's like you're buying the same shit over and over again, just different pitch tones and voices and shit like that. It's not only the rappers trying to be another rapper, [but also] he got the same producers, so it's like you hear the same music and you hear the same fucking song over and over again. As opposed to [in the golden age, where] the same people that love Rakim love G Rap and vice versa, *but* G Rap and Rakim was totally different. Same people that love G Rap, love Big Daddy Kane, love KRS-One, love Chuck D, love EPMD, but nobody can say, "Yo, their shit sound all the same." So that's how the rappers today differ from the rappers in the golden era of hip-hop—there's [less] variety, the same type of shit over and over again, just different groups.[31]

Pigeon John

There's less characters . . . there's pretty much two types of MC nowadays, there's the "I just got out of the coke game" MC and the "I want some ass tonight, I want to get drunk. . . ." So there's two types of MCs nowadays, and they all look the same too—I mean the guy can be from Brooklyn and look like he's from Atlanta or from Santa Ana, or from Miami, all of them look the same. The beats sound the same for the most part. And there's definitely following and not leading, so I think it's just a dog chasing its tail nowadays. But once in a while, for me, there's some incredible stuff, like once in a while, for me, the magic is still there. But back in the day you had a Slick Rick, you had A Tribe Called Quest, you had a De La Soul, you had a Beastie Boys, you had a Public Enemy—they had Public Enemy and the Beastie Boys on the same tour! Nowadays you have [two artists] on the same tour, it's the same guy, they're the same people, you can switch them out. So I think the personality is gone.[32]

Bobby Creekwater

Today's MCs . . . this is my only gripe, I just wish a lot more MCs would come into it with their own identity. I think MCs of the past, everybody had their own niche and their own thing and nowadays you get some MCs going for the same approach or doing the same type of music. Even if it's subconscious, they end up doing the same type of music or what have you. Back when everybody was on their own thing, it was exciting because of it, like the anticipation level as a fan was higher, nowadays it's like, nothing much to look for.[33]

Focus on Hit Singles and Commercialization

Although hip-hop had hit singles and catchy choruses during the golden age, it became increasingly more and more reliant on a hit formula in order to gain wider attention. This again led to a lack of inventiveness, as artists strived to find a hit rather than experimenting with new approaches and sounds.

R.A. The Rugged Man

Any time anything becomes commercialized, it becomes diluted. It doesn't matter if it's film, art, music, anything, as soon as something becomes a commercial art form, you lose it, it becomes diluted and it becomes a money thing rather than an artistic thing. [Nowadays, record labels] don't even want to market hip-hop in any way, they just wanna go, "Okay, what songs will a little kid sing in elementary schools, what songs will fifty-year-old mothers sing with their little kids," rather than, "let's make a real hip-hop record."[34]

Termanology

It's a different game, it's changed, it's a lot more dumbed down now and everybody's trying to sound the same, which is understandable, because everybody is trying to get on the radio. You basically gotta sound like what's going on to get on. Back in the days it was way better, man, because everybody just had their own style. You could come out screaming, you could come out like Busta Rhymes if you wanted to, you could come out like however, but now everybody's just trying to be the same, and that's the wack shit about back in the days versus now.[35]

During the golden age, rappers and groups were able to find a balance between being commercial enough to gain radio and video play, while still maintaining a high level of creativity and complexity. Many feel that this was lost after the end of the golden age.

GZA, Wu-Tang Clan

Nowadays it seems like it's cool to be dumb. MCs were a whole lot more lyrical back then, like Rakim. . . . That's what MCing is about. Not being commercial and watered down or gimmicky. [Big Daddy] Kane was doing lyrical songs that were hard and commercial. A lot of cats from that era were very lyrical. You can name at least ten MCs back then that was in the spotlight at the same time that was all lyrical and all different. Try to name ten now in the spotlight. They are all similar. Everyone is following and biting. No one is really writing anything lyrically profound. We are giving MCs the title of greatest and they [aren't] lyrically skilled like that. Come on now.[36]

Harder to Sample

The production sound of the golden age faced a big setback toward the end of the time period, due to artists being sued over sampling. As sampling formed the basis of the musical aesthetic, this meant that it was far harder to experiment with the art form—beatmakers had to be wary of how much they were sampling and how they were using the samples.

Mike Simpson

You could do it as an art project, if somebody gave you a couple million dollars to make a record like [Beastie Boys's *Paul's Boutique*, which was built on many samples], but commercially, I don't think you could ever do it again.[37]

Dave, De La Soul

["Transmitting Live from Mars" was] the one that the Turtles sued us for. It startled us at the time, because we were clueless about how severe it could get. The attacks [lawsuits], especially the Turtles one, started coming after the record went gold.[38]

One particularly prominent case had a huge impact—in 1991, Biz Markie's song "Alone Again" sampled portions of "Alone Again (Naturally)" by Gilbert O'Sullivan. The judgment in this case essentially resulted in all future hip-hop albums having to clear all of the samples they used to avoid a lawsuit. Biz Markie titled his follow-up album *All Samples Cleared!* in reference to the court decision.

Tyrone Williams, Cold Chillin' Records Chairman

This is a reactionary business. With the Biz [Markie] case everybody went sample clearance crazy [and] now you pay so much for samples that the balance is gonna end up zero anyway. Everyone is so fearful now, and you have people out there who are like scavengers who can't wait to hear something and take it overboard.[39]

9. Landmark Albums in Hip-Hop History

Hip-hop's history can be summarized through several landmark albums. These records illustrate hip-hop's evolution and provide examples of hip-hop's sound during specific stages of its development.

Various Artists—*Wild Style* Original Soundtrack (1983)

Much of hip-hop's old-school era (more on p. 133) was based around singles rather than albums, or not recorded at all—hip-hop started in the early 1970s, but the first widely released rap records did not appear until 1979.

However, the sound track to the film *Wild Style* from 1983 is one of the few examples of an essential old-school album that gives a feel of the style and the scene. It works from beginning to end as an album, rather than just as a collection of singles, and it features performances from artists who otherwise aren't heard often on record, such as Grandmaster Caz (see p. 76) and Grand Wizard Theodore (see p. 136).

Charlie Ahearn

Wild Style was blessed with incredible musical talent. I tried to embrace as wide a picture of Bronx hip-hop stars as could fit into our little movie. . . . Like Busy Bee as the cut up MC in the Alps Hotel scene, Double Trouble on The Stoop. Grand Wizzard Theodore and The Fantastic 5, The Cold Crush Brothers were the big rivals then, since Flash and The Furious were out on tour with Sugarhill. I got the inspiration from watching street ball at the West 4th spot to pit the two crews against each other in a live match. The rival MCs took that scene as a life and death match and they were right. We are still watching them today to see who is stronger. I was also inspired by the lyrical chops of my friend Grandmaster Caz of the Cold Crush. . . . Later, when we were putting together the soundtrack album. . . . I wanted Caz to write the movie's theme and then record it. . . . He rhymes [it] a cappella in the movie.[1]

Grandmaster Caz

Say what you want about *Wild Style*, but it's the first and the best, and no Hollywood movie has been able to capture the realism, the times, and the energy that created this multi-billion dollar industry better.[2]

Rather than rapping over popular hits of the time, original backing music was created for the movie and the sound track and handed out to various DJs. This gave the sound track the same general sound of that era, where rappers rapped over records, but it also set it apart by supplying never-before-heard compositions to rap over.

Fab 5 Freddy

I was ready to use the music exactly as it was used at the parties, but Charlie [Ahearn] had the great foresight to say (and this was way before anyone knew the word "sampling"), "Hey, people own the rights to this music, and if we just use it, we could get in trouble at some point." Probably not at that point, because the music was very obscure and the hip-hop world had not become this billion-dollar global industry. Charlie suggested, "We should come up with our own music," and I agreed. I wanted to make the equivalent of break beat records that the DJs in our film could use and mix to create the musical bed that rappers would rhyme over. That would become our soundtrack. I had never produced anything, so I figured it out as we went along. I got David Harpur to play bass, Chris Stein to play guitar, and Lenny Ferraro, who was part of the *TV Party* Orchestra, to play drums. We had twelve short songs . . . every DJ that was involved in the film got two copies of that record. That's [Grandmaster] Flash, [Grandwizard] Theodore, Charlie Chase, Tony Tone, and DJ AJ.[3]

The sound track, along with the movie itself, has been sampled by a lot of later hip-hop artists, and it continues to be a source of inspiration for many, cementing its reputation as one of the cornerstones of the old-school era.

Cut Chemist, Jurassic 5

Wild Style has been the old school reference point for me and my music for over twenty years. I often go back to this film to channel the spirit of true street and visual performance art. It is a product of its time: the early '80s, when bridges were crossed between genres and styles, between rich and poor.[4]

Fab 5 Freddy

Nas used [parts of *Wild Style*] on his record, [and so did] the Beastie Boys. Many cats did. Nas' first album, the classic

Illmatic, opens up with the scene from *Wild Style* where Zoro's brother, home from the army, disses his art. Nas [changes it around so that it's] like *he's* the kid his brother is dissing.[5]

Charlie Ahearn

If sampling is the most sincere form of flattery, then *Wild Style* has gotten plenty of love in the past 25 years: Nas, Beastie Boys, Biz Markie, Jurassic 5, the list goes on and on.[6]

Run-D.M.C.—*Run-D.M.C.* (1984)

Run-D.M.C.'s debut was monumental in several respects. As we saw in chapter 7, it ended the old-school era of hip-hop with its new sound and style, and in chapter 5 we saw how Larry Smith's groundbreaking production contributed to its impact. It broke new ground in other ways as well.

Most hip-hop albums up until that point had been centered around a couple of hit singles, which meant the rest of the album was often filler or attempts at re-creating the hits. Run-D.M.C.'s debut took more of its cue from classic rock albums, making each song count and work as part of the album as a whole.

Bill Adler

[Russell Simmons] and Larry [Smith] had cooked up a pretty ambitious plan. The typical rap album then consisted of a hit single or two and a lot of filler. Production-wise, the trend was simply to recycle somebody else's work—Chic's "Good Times," the Tom Tom Club's "Genius of Love," Taana Gardner's "Heartbeat," Queen's "Another One Bites the Dust," and others. Run-D.M.C.'s debut album would break the mold: nine songs, all of them originals, and every one a winner.[7]

The album also fused hip-hop with rock on the song "Rock Box," featuring guitar riffs from rock guitarist Eddie Martinez. This fusion predates many later successful combinations of rock and rap by groups such as Rage Against the Machine, Cypress Hill, and artists who were part of the late '90s rap-rock and rap-metal movements.

Russell Simmons

Rap is the outlaw black music, and rock is the outlaw white music. Two opposites together as one. [Run-D.M.C.] saw these loud guitars [used by a hard-rock band at the studio they were recording in] and they started screaming, "We can do that! What the fuck—we're going to make loud shit, too!"[8]

Eddie Martinez

[It was multitracked, layered guitars], I'd say there are close to ten guitar tracks on ["Rock Box"].[9]

As rappers, Run and D.M.C. used hard-hitting, direct vocals that perfectly suited the music they were rapping over—this more aggressive style helped to further enhance the overall image they presented.

Kool Moe Dee

My love, understanding, and appreciation for Run-D.M.C. came after the heat and the hype was over. In retrospect I understood how important they were as MCs. The musical impact was obvious. As a group they set the tone for hip-hop to be the multi-billion dollar industry that it is today. Most people thought that D.M.C. was the more lyrical of the two, [though] Run was the more dynamic. [Run] has one of the most recognizable voices in the history of hip-hop . . . those rock 'n' roll records would not have worked without Run's vocal energy. By 1986, Run-D.M.C. was the benchmark for everything in hip-hop.[10]

Eric B. & Rakim—*Paid in Full* (1987)

Paid in Full combines some of the biggest developments in rapping by Rakim (see p. 80), with cutting-edge beatmaking, made in part by legendary beatmaker Marley Marl (see p. 98). The album pushed both elements forward simultaneously, making it one of the most lauded and influential albums in hip-hop history.

As well as his widely acknowledged breakthroughs in rap's rhythms and rhymes (see p. 81), Rakim also had sophisticated lyrical content—rather than using straightforward braggadocio, he would refer to scientists, poets, and philosophers, adding a level of intricacy that rewarded the listener on repeated listens. He combined this level of intelligence with a hard, street feel, a combination that has had a big influence on many other rappers.

50 Cent
I remember hearing [Rakim's] music way back, on *Paid in Full*. Rakim was way ahead of his time when he came out. He was able to stay street-oriented while being intelligent. He seemed more intelligent than the rest of the other artists out there that were just rapping. Everything about him, his whole swagger, him as a person, is what made that work, and he made other MCs come up behind him and

follow in his footsteps so hard. He gave birth to Nas, damn near. Nas is dope, though. Style-wise, Rakim influenced that.[11]

Nas

Eric B. and Rakim epitomized and personified the street culture of New York and the rest of the nation. They wore Gucci before Gucci [was popular in the streets], they were counting money on the album cover and they made it look cool. The style of the music was built for the streets. Rakim's lyrics were the streets put into music.[12]

While Rakim's influence on rapping is rarely contested, there is uncertainty over who was responsible for the state-of-the-art beats, which also had a big impact on later hip-hop. While Eric B. and Rakim are listed as producers of the album, Marley Marl is known to have programmed some of the tracks, giving them the new, hard, sampled sound that he had pioneered (see p. 98). Part of this disagreement over credit for the production revolves around the imprecise nature of the term *producer*.

Rakim

I did most of the production [on the Eric B. & Rakim albums] . . . "Eric B Is President" [for example]. My man Eric put the bassline on though. "My Melody," but Marley [Marl] did it at his crib. That was early. It was my idea. I could keep going man, [I produced] damn near everything, "I Ain't No Joke," "Move the Crowd."[13]

Eric B.

[Marley Marl] was the engineer of the session, not the producer of the session. I took the records to Marley Marl's house in Queensbridge and paid Marley Marl to be the engineer. That's why he's not a producer, that's why he is not getting publishing. I brought the music. I just couldn't work the equipment, because that's not what I did. Marley can't tell you where he got the records from. I brought the records with me, I knew what I wanted.[14]

Marley Marl

A lot of times people . . . come with an idea: "I wanna use so-and-so for my record." So my job was to go get so-and-so and hook it up the best way it could. I always say the proof is in the pudding. If you think you made it, when you make your album, if it don't come out like the shit I did, [then] everybody's gonna know that [you didn't make the beats]. My perception of a producer is the [person] that makes the track. Whose hands made it? They did it. Because me and you could sit here together and we could sample the same [track], but that's not to say we're gonna make the same [record from it]. There's a certain feeling that you put on it and that's what makes you a producer. That's who produces the record—whoever puts the feeling on that track. Not the person saying, "Okay, I wanna use this." Okay, you brought the idea up front, but the actual person putting it down, putting it in the computer, is producing it.[15]

Public Enemy—*It Takes a Nation of Millions to Hold Us Back* (1988)

As well as its groundbreaking production by the Bomb Squad (see p. 103), Public Enemy's 1988 release, *It Takes a Nation of Millions to Hold Us Back*, included the distinct, forceful vocals of lead rapper Chuck D, who cut through the densely layered sample collages.

Kool Moe Dee

Chuck D is the greatest voice in hip-hop history. There has never been a greater voice in hip-hop, figuratively or literally. . . . His voice and his delivery are the equivalent of an explosion. His voice is the main thing within the chaotic, loud, sonic music, and the music can't drown him out.[16]

Chuck D made political content the focus throughout the album, covering it in more depth than any rapper before him—the record remains the benchmark for measuring politically themed hip-hop.

Ice Cube

Chuck D—he's my No. 1, because his music was life changing. His music wasn't just rapping. It was more than that.[17]

Chuck D, Public Enemy

We wanted to be a social critic, a community voice. We wanted everyone to know, truly understand, that our music was from the people, not above the people. "Don't Believe the Hype," without question, still speaks volumes. To me it is Noam Chomsky–like in its theme and content. Like Chomsky does with his work, "Don't Believe the Hype" addresses media disinformation and picks it apart.[18]

It Takes a Nation also continued the path laid by Run-D.M.C.'s debut—the songs enhanced each other, presenting a unified message and worldview. It worked as a coherent album with strong themes and aesthetics, rather than just as a collection of singles.

Chuck D, Public Enemy

We wanted to make a *What's Going On* [by Marvin Gaye] of rap music and we set out to make it with those intentions. We wanted to look at the album format the same way the

Beatles looked at *Sgt. Pepper*, the same way Earth, Wind & Fire looked at *Gratitude* and *That's the Way of the World*. We had a sensibility of what it took to make an album from an album standpoint and leave the singles as something that peppered it, but didn't saturate it. We didn't want to make a record that went cut to cut. We wanted to put some different "interstitials" as they say in the television world. We wanted a live effect like *Gratitude* from Earth, Wind, & Fire. I had a tape of where we just played in London to a raucous crowd, so we interspersed that between the cuts to show people we had a live element to us. We had to get it all out in one album.[19]

The album also benefited from the input and performances of rapper Flavor Flav, who acted as a comic foil to Chuck D, ad-libbing humorous short phrases and words around Chuck's verses, as well as providing the main vocals for "Cold Lampin' with Flavor."

Nas

It was something like I've never heard before. Chuck D's voice and what he was saying made me think. Flavor Flav's voice, his attitude, and how he supported Chuck [was dope]. And the beats by the Bomb Squad were out of this world. Public Enemy took a strong position as a leader in the music community. They were brave.[20]

It is often cited as the best hip-hop album of all time by music magazines such as *NME*, *Vibe*, and *Q*, due to the combination of groundbreaking beats, the vocal power of Chuck D, the extensive social commentary, and the conceptual nature of the album.

N.W.A.—*Straight Outta Compton* (1988)

While there were gangsta rap themes and content on earlier hip-hop records, dealing with violence, crime, and inner-city life, N.W.A.'s *Straight Outta Compton* was the album that made gangsta rap a huge and commercially viable subgenre of hip-hop. It is the quintessential gangsta rap record which catapulted the more controversial and aggressive elements of hip-hop to the forefront.

James Lavelle, UNKLE

[*Straight Outta Compton*] was the punk hip-hop record of its generation: it changed everything about the way you looked at hip-hop. It was anarchy, and the impact it's had on hip-hop in general—the way that rap as a language changed—was unbelievable. It's a very historically important record in the same way that [the Sex Pistols's] *Never Mind the Bollocks* was for what it did for youth culture, the attitude, the image, the production, everything. I first heard it on a bootleg tape and it was one of those records that spread like wildfire.[21]

Akrobatik

N.W.A. . . . . they were like the flagship gangsta rap artists . . . everyone during this period just wanted to have that gangster swagger and put out drug dealer gangster music.[22]

MURS

No one saw gangsta rap coming. They told them they were crazy: You're gonna curse on a record and it's gonna get played? Yeah, right! And now everything on the radio [is like that]. They changed the world [and] you couldn't have told anyone. . . . [23]

Rick Rubin

I remember hearing the song "Straight Outta Compton" for the first time and I couldn't believe it. Loved it. And I remember going to see them play. I think it was in Inglewood. It was the first time I saw a lot of guns in hip-hop. Before N.W.A. went out on stage, a guy came around with towels, and he opened up the towels and there were loaded guns. And everybody got loaded up to go out on stage. It was unbelievable. And I remember Eazy-E walking around backstage watching a portable TV and holding a machine gun.[24]

They presented themselves as "the world's most dangerous group," so to many listeners N.W.A. appeared and sounded like an authentic Los Angeles gang who had made a record. Their larger-than-life tales were cinematic, exciting, and often exaggeratedly overblown—obviously fictional when scrutinized, but still highly entertaining to their audience.

Dr. Dre

Living up to what you say on records . . . it's all entertainment. Anybody in their fucking right mind knows you can talk about shooting somebody on a record, but [somebody isn't going to] really go out there and do it, unless you're just stupid. It's entertainment, you know, we make records, it's entertainment, that's all it is. This is like our fucking jobs.[25]

The album combined dense, funky, and sometimes chaotic beats from Dr. Dre, one of hip-hop's most successful producers, with the rhymes of Ice Cube, MC Ren, and the late Eazy-E, along with production input from DJ Yella.

Kokane

Watching them make those N.W.A. records was really something. Dre is a phenomenal dude. All of those collective people made those projects all the way down to the bass player. . . . You had to be there to really understand what that magic was all about. It was amazing to witness that sort of energy at a time when it was still fresh like the Beatles had once been. It was mass mania, man! I mean, it was bananas, homie. There will never be another N.W.A. in the same way that there will never be another 2Pac; there will never be another Eazy[-E].[26]

The Beastie Boys—
Paul's Boutique
(1989)

Similar in its sampling diversity to the work of producer Prince Paul on De La Soul's *3 Feet High and Rising* (see p. 107), the Beastie Boys's *Paul's Boutique* is credited as one of the key albums that took sampling further than it had ever been taken before. With input from the Beastie Boys, the bulk of the production was handled by the production duo of Mike Simpson and John King, better known as the Dust Brothers, along with label owner Matt Dike.

MCA, the Beastie Boys

[The Dust Brothers] had a bunch of music together, before we arrived to work with them. As a result, a lot of the tracks on *Paul's Boutique* come from songs they'd planned to release to clubs as instrumentals, "Shake Your Rump," for example. They'd put together some beats, basslines and guitar lines, all these loops together, and they were quite surprised when we said we wanted to rhyme on it, because they thought it was too dense. They offered to strip it down to just beats, but we wanted all of that stuff on there. I think half of the tracks were written when we got there, and the other half we wrote together.[27]

Mike Simpson, the Dust Brothers

We were just putting together instrumental tracks, not knowing who they were for. And every day, a different rapper would come in—Tone-Loc, Young MC, Def Jeff. I think it was sorta like the old Motown days, where they recorded the tracks, and then had all the artists come in and try to do a vocal on it. And whoever did the best one got the track. [Some tracks,] they were these crazy mega-mixes, that had tons of samples, tons of scratching. A lot of them were so dense that there really wasn't room for a rapper on the track. We would try with Loc, and we would try with Young MC, but there just wasn't room for anything. And they were a little weirder than the other stuff we were doing. So we just put those aside as Dust Brothers tracks. And we guessed at some point, we'd have enough to make a record.[28] Then the Beastie Boys wandered into the studio, and heard one of these tracks, and they loved it. That's how the album got started.[29]

Paul's Boutique was one of only a small number of records at the time that was layered and densely packed with samples, as opposed to a minimal collection of sounds.

Mike Simpson, the Dust Brothers

Up until that point in hip-hop, people had been using samples very sparsely and minimally. If anything, they would use one sample in a song and take a drum loop and that would be the foundation. But what we were doing was making entire songs out of samples taken from various dif-

ferent sources. On *Paul's Boutique* everything was a collage.
There was one track on which the Beastie Boys played some
instruments, but apart from that everything was made of
samples. But we never had a grand vision of trying to make
groundbreaking music. We just enjoyed making music in a
way that was an extension of our DJing, combining two or
three songs, but with greater accuracy than you could do with
turntables. People asked us why our stuff from the late 1980s
sounded so good, and we said that it simply was because the
original recordings that we sampled sounded so good.[30]

MCA, the Beastie Boys

It all sounded incredible. It was so rich with layer upon
layer of music.[31]

The album also drew from an incredibly diverse range of records,
as opposed to staples from genres such as funk and soul that many
other hip-hop producers relied on.

Mike Simpson, the Dust Brothers

We were mixing shit like Black Oak Arkansas with Sly &
the Family Stone, or Alice Cooper with the Crash Crew . . .
we were looking to produce edgier, more emotional records that would sound a little different each time you heard
them. We filled 24-track tapes with loops and scratches
running all the way through . . . the people who worked at
the studios thought we were crazy at the time, 'cause they
had never seen anybody make songs that way.[32]

Tim Carr

[Before *Paul's Boutique* and De La Soul's *3 Feet High and
Rising*], all samples were from a small, select set of break-
beats that you fucked with at your own risk.[33]

Mike D, the Beastie Boys

[On "High Plains Drifter"] Matt and I just thought it was hilarious, sampling the Eagles [song, "Those Shoes"] . . . you wouldn't have thought an Eagles record would have this incredible beat.[34]

Due to the extreme range and density of the sample collages on the record, complemented by the Beastie Boys's similarly diverse range of lyrical references and allusions, it is often held up as one of the pinnacles of sample innovation. It is also an album that would be difficult to produce today, given the more stringent nature of current sampling laws.

Young MC

Paul's Boutique was the greatest sampling record ever.[35]

A Tribe Called Quest— *The Low End Theory* (1991)

Released in 1991, A Tribe Called Quest's second album, *The Low End Theory*, is considered a high point, arguably *the* high point, of jazz-rap and known for its highbrow and more "intellectual" overall sound.

Bob Power

The Low End Theory was an interesting record; in a way, it was [the Beatles'] *Sgt. Pepper's* of hip-hop. It's a record that changed the way that people thought about putting music together.[36]

Nas

I felt like [A Tribe Called Quest's first album], *People's Instinctive Travels*, was a crazy album. But they evolved on *The Low End Theory*. It was already dope shit on the first album, but the second album took it to a broader audience and they stepped it up even higher which I didn't even think could be possible. It's just one of those records that just took everybody by storm.[37]

Although it wasn't the first record to fuse jazz with hip-hop (either through samples or stylistic rapping techniques), it is often seen as the peak of the marriage between hip-hop and jazz.

Q-Tip, A Tribe Called Quest

When it came to hip-hop and jazz, the work we were doing was a unique opportunity to combine both of them, like the way we used [jazz bassist] Ron Carter on "Verses from the Abstract." Both musics came from the black underclass, and both are very expressive. There were so many similarities, and that made it even better to sample it and rhyme over it.[38]

Prince Paul

Tribe's *Low End Theory* used this awesome track called "Star of a Story" off Heatwave's *Central Heating* album. I thought about using that but they used it in such a good, slick way that I didn't dare touch it! The different types of records they used and just how many layers they placed and where they placed was just so crazy. The [record] digging they do is insane.[39]

Adding bass played by legendary jazz musician Ron Carter also helped to introduce a mix of live musicianship into wider hip-hop production, to complement the samples.

Bob Power

Q-Tip [of A Tribe Called Quest] had a bass-line riff from a record that he wanted Ron [Carter] to play. Ron sketched it out on staff paper and went into the booth. He started playing, and a couple of notes weren't right. [We] all looked at each other, and were all like, "No, you tell him." This is Ron Carter, after all. We were all shaking in our boots, but I went in and said, "Ron, look, the last 16th note, it's an Eb, not a Bb." And he simply said, "Okay," and played it right. We were worried about Ron being a bit prickly, but discovered that he's really just a super-pro working musician.[40]

As well as the skillful blending of jazz and hip-hop, the record was also known for bringing improved sonic clarity to hip-hop, with the help of acclaimed engineer and producer Bob Power.

Mr. Walt, Da Beatminerz

Bob Power, one of the most incredible engineers ever to get on a board, he just did his thing on there, and just made it incredible. The way they did that record—wow.[41]

Bob Power

I also spent a lot of time on *The Low End Theory* taking extraneous noise out of the samples . . . which is one of the reasons why it sounds very dimensional. If you listen, you won't hear a lot of surface noise, crackles, or pops. Back then, we didn't have software that did it, so I did all sorts of nutty things. Among other things, I used an esoteric piece of gear called the Burwyn Noise Eliminator, and some high-end home stereo components that took clicks and pops out.[42]

Notes

1. What Is Hip-Hop?

(Regarding interviews by author: audio recordings and transcripts from author's private archives.)

1. JayQuan, "Remembering Keith Cowboy," The Foundation, 2005, http://thafoundation.com/cowboy.htm.
2. *Just to Get a Rep*, directed by Peter Gerard (Edinburgh: Accidental Media, 2004), DVD.
3. Alex Nino Gheciu, "Revolutionaries Month: A Q&A with the Godfather of Hip-Hop, Afrika Bambaataa," Aux, October 12, 2011, http://www.aux.tv/2011/10/revolutionaries-month-a-qa-with-the-godfather-of-hip-hop-afrika-bambaataa/.
4. *Just to Get a Rep*, directed by Peter Gerard (Edinburgh: Accidental Media, 2004), DVD.
5. Lord Jamar, interview by author, March 26, 2007.
6. Buckshot, interview by author, May 15, 2007.
7. Slava Kuperstein, "DJ Premier on Kanye's New Album: 'Strictly Hard Beats and Rhymes,'" *HipHopDX*, April 12, 2010, http://www.hiphopdx.com/index/news/id.11017/title.dj-premier-on-kanyes-new-album-strictly-hard-beats-and-rhymes.
8. riotsound.com, "Hip-Hop, Rap Interviews: Tha Alkaholiks,"

accessed February 10, 2013, http://www.riotsound.com/hip
-hop/rap/interviews/The-Alkaholiks/index.php.

9. Paul Meara, "Inspectah Deck Says Esoteric Is 'Up There' with
Eminem & CZARFACE Is a 'Friendly Duel,'" *HipHopDX*,
February 11, 2013, http://www.hiphopdx.com/index/inter
views/id.2040/title.inspectah-deck-says-esoteric-is-up-there
-with-eminem-czarface-is-a-friendly-duel-.

10. Tech N9ne, interview by author, March 27, 2008.

11. Rah Digga, interview by author, May 6, 2008.

12. *The MC: Why We Do It*, directed by Peter Spirer (United States:
QD3 Entertainment, 2005), DVD.

13. One Be Lo, interview by author, March 12, 2007.

14. *The MC: Why We Do It*, directed by Peter Spirer (United States:
QD3 Entertainment, 2005), DVD.

15. Ibid.

16. Ibid.

17. Antonino D'Ambrosio, "Interview: Chuck D," the *Progressive*, August 2005, http://progressive.org/mag_chuckd.

18. Tech N9ne, interview by author, March 27, 2008.

19. Del the Funky Homosapien, Interview by author, October 14,
2007.

20. Shook G, interview by author, October 3, 2007.

21. *The Freshest Kids*, directed by Israel (QD3 Entertainment,
2002), DVD.

22. Alex Nino Gheciu, "Revolutionaries Month: A Q&A with the
Godfather of Hip-Hop, Afrika Bambaataa," Aux, October 12,
2011, http://www.aux.tv/2011/10/revolutionaries-month-a-qa
-with-the-godfather-of-hip-hop-afrika-bambaataa/.

23. *Just to Get a Rep*, directed by Peter Gerard (Edinburgh: Accidental Media, 2004), DVD.

24. Jeff Chang, *Can't Stop Won't Stop: A History of the Hip-Hop
Generation* (New York: Picador, 2005), 193.

25. Jim Fricke and Charlie Ahearn, *Yes Yes Y'all: The Experience*

Music Project Oral History of Hip-Hop's First Decade (New York: Da Capo, 2002), 337.

26. Andrew J. Rausch, *I Am Hip-Hop: Conversations on the Music and Culture* (Lanham, MD: Scarecrow, 2011), 131.

27. *Just to Get a Rep,* directed by Peter Gerard (Edinburgh: Accidental Media, 2004), DVD.

28. Ibid.

29. Nelson George, "Hip-Hop's Founding Fathers Speak the Truth," *That's the Joint!: The Hip-Hop Studies Reader,* eds. Murray Forman and Mark Anthony Neal (New York: Routledge, 2004), 46.

30. *Just to Get a Rep,* directed by Peter Gerard (Edinburgh: Accidental Media, 2004), DVD.

31. Michael A. Gonzales, "Enter 'Wild Style,' 30 Years Later," Ebony.com, September 27, 2013, http://www.ebony.com/entertainment-culture/vintage-vision-enter-the-wild-style-393.

32. *New York* magazine, "Graffiti in Its Own Words," January 22, 2013, http://nymag.com/guides/summer/17406/index4.html.

33. Ibid.

34. *Just to Get a Rep,* directed by Peter Gerard (Edinburgh: Accidental Media, 2004), DVD.

35. JayQuan, "Interview with Charlie Ahearn, Director of Hip-Hop Classic Film," The Foundation, May 3, 2004, http://www.thafoundation.com/charliea.htm.

36. Jeff Chang, *Can't Stop Won't Stop: A History of the Hip-Hop Generation* (New York: Picador, 2005), 111.

37. *Just to Get a Rep,* directed by Peter Gerard (Edinburgh: Accidental Media, 2004), DVD.

38. *New York* magazine, "Graffiti in Its Own Words," January 22, 2013, http://nymag.com/guides/summer/17406/index4.html.

39. *Just to Get a Rep,* directed by Peter Gerard (Edinburgh: Accidental Media, 2004), DVD.

40. Adam Mansbach, "Poetic Injustice: Hip Hop Pioneer Phase 2,"

January 23, 2013, http://adammansbach.com/other/phase
.html.

41. Joe Austin, *Taking the Train* (New York: Columbia University Press, 2001), 203.

42. Paine, "Fuzz One: No Mistakes Allowed," Allhiphop.com, April 11, 2006, http://allhiphop.com/2006/04/11/fuzz-one -no-mistakes-allowed/.

43. *Just to Get a Rep*, directed by Peter Gerard (Edinburgh: Accidental Media, 2004), DVD.

44. Alice Muir, "Lady Pink Interview," *TLG Magazine*, January 2, 2013, http://tlgmagazine.com/interview-lady-pink/.

45. Troy Smith, "An Interview with Buddy Esquire, 'the Flyer King,'" Oldschoolhip-hop.com, October 5, 2010, http://www .oldschoolhiphop.com/interviews/buddyesquire.htm.

46. Joe Austin, *Taking the Train* (New York: Columbia University Press, 2001), 206.

47. Joseph G. Schloss, *Foundation: B-boys, B-girls and Hip-Hop Culture in New York* (New York: Oxford University Press, 2009), 31.

48. Ibid., 17.

49. Jim Fricke and Charlie Ahearn, *Yes Yes Y'all: The Experience Music Project Oral History of Hip-Hop's First Decade* (New York: Da Capo, 2002), 337.

50. Mike Gadd and Gerald Ward II (Whiz), "Living Legend: Afrika Bambaataa," Zulu Nation September 2003, http:// www.zulunation.nl/index.php/geschiedenis/the-founder /205-living-legend-afrika-bambaataa.html.

51. K-Os, interview by author, April 26, 2007.

52. Big Noyd, interview by author, March 25, 2008.

53. Kool G Rap, interview by author, October 30, 2007.

54. Zmex, interview by author, May 3, 2007.

55. Akir, interview by author, March 29, 2007.

56. Lord Jamar, interview by author, March 26, 2007.

57. Tech N9ne, interview by author, March 27, 2008.

58. Planet Asia, interview by author, June 6, 2007.

59. Questlove, "When the People Cheer: How Hip-Hop Failed Black America," Vulture, 22 April, 2014, http://www.vulture .com/2014/04/questlove-on-how-hip-hop-failed-black -america.html.

2. Hip-Hop Music Appreciation

1. *Something from Nothing: The Art of Rap*, directed by Ice-T and Andy Baybutt (London: Kaleidoscope Home Entertainment, 2012), DVD.

2. Evidence, interview by author, February 11, 2008.

3. HalftimeOnline, "Big Daddy Kane," March 17, 2004, http:// halftimeonline.net/portfolio/big-daddy-kane/.

4. Shock G, interview by author, September 9, 2012.

5. Aesop Rock, interview by author, April 21, 2008.

6. Del the Funky Homosapien, interview by author, December 11, 2012.

7. Royce Da 5'9", interview by author, May 14, 2008.

8. Masta Ace, interview by author, April 24, 2007.

9. Gift of Gab, interview by author, September 20, 2007.

10. *Something from Nothing: The Art of Rap*, directed by Ice-T and Andy Baybutt (London: Kaleidoscope Home Entertain-ment, 2012), DVD.

11. Masta Ace, interview by author, April 24, 2007.

12. ComplexTV, "Magnum Opus" February 15, 2013, http:// www.complex.com/tv/shows/magnum-opus.

13. Big Daddy Kane, interview by author, March 31, 2008.

14. Myka 9, interview by author, May 16, 2007.

15. Busta Nut, "Ya Heard? E-40 Invented Every Rap Word You Ever Heard," Vice.com, November 30, 2002, http:// www.vice.com/read/ya-v9n7.

16. Myka 9, interview by author, May 16, 2007.

17. Tech N9ne, interview by author, March 27, 2008.

18. HalftimeOnline, "Mele Mel," March 5, 2013, http://half timeonline.net/mele-mel/.

19. Brother J, interview by author, February 20, 2007.

20. Sean Price, interview by author, May 18, 2007.

21. Crooked I, interview by author, April 23, 2008.

22. Kembrew McLeod and Peter DiCola, *Creative License: The Law and Culture of Digital Sampling* (Durham, NC: Duke University Press, 2011), 101.

23. Joe Fassler, "How Copyright Law Hurts Music, From Chuck D to Girl Talk," April 12, 2011, the *Atlantic*, http://www.the atlantic.com/entertainment/archive/2011/04/how-copyright -law-hurts-music-from-chuck-d-to-girl-talk/236975/.

24. Andrew Mason, "Pete Rock Reminisces," *Wax Poetics*, Issue 7, Winter 2004.

25. Andre Torres, "The Architect," *Scratch Magazine*, Issue 1, Summer 2004, p. 76

26. Eliot Wilder, *Endtroducing . . .* (New York: Continuum, 2005), 89.

27. Kembrew McLeod and Peter DiCola, *Creative License: The Law and Culture of Digital Sampling* (Durham, NC: Duke University Press, 2011), 24.

28. Joseph G. Schloss, *Making Beats: The Art of Sample-Based Hip-Hop* (Middletown, CT: Wesleyan University Press, 2004), 164–165.

29. Kembrew McLeod and Peter DiCola, *Creative License: The Law and Culture of Digital Sampling* (Durham, NC: Duke University Press, 2011), 24.

30. Eliot Wilder, *Endtroducing . . .* (New York: Continuum, 2005), 71.

31. Kembrew McLeod and Peter DiCola, *Creative License: The Law and Culture of Digital Sampling* (Durham, NC: Duke University Press, 2011), 20.

32. Joseph G. Schloss, *Making Beats: The Art of Sample-Based Hip-Hop* (Middletown, CT: Wesleyan University Press, 2004), 67.
33. Nate Patrin, "Interviews: Steinski," *Pitchfork*, August 26, 2008, http://pitchfork.com/features/interviews/7149-steinski/.
34. Agent B, "Cut Chemist Interview," *Oh Word*, December 13, 2006, http://archive.ohword.com/features/543/cut-chemist -interview.

3. Debunking Hip-Hop Myths

1. Jim Fricke and Charlie Ahearn, *Yes Yes Y'all: The Experience Music Project Oral History of Hip-Hop's First Decade* (New York: Da Capo, 2002), 90.
2. Joseph G. Schloss, *Making Beats: The Art of Sample-Based Hip-Hop* (Middletown, CT: Wesleyan University Press, 2004), 30.
3. Ibid., 29.
4. Jerry L. Barrow, "Large Professor: Revolve Around Science," Nodfactor.com, September 29, 2008, http://www.nodfactor .com/2008/09/29/large-professor-revolve-around-science/.
5. Joseph G. Schloss, *Making Beats: The Art of Sample-Based Hip-Hop* (Middletown, CT: Wesleyan University Press, 2004), 29.
6. Ibid.
7. Mark Katz, *Groove Music: The Art and Culture of the Hip-Hop DJ* (New York: Oxford University Press, 2012), 41.
8. Bill Adler, *Tougher Than Leather: The Rise of Run-DMC* (Los Angeles: Consafos Press, 2002), 44.
9. Ibid., 44–45.
10. Stephen Webber, *DJ Skills: The Essential Guide to Mixing and Scratching* (Burlington, MA: Focal Press, 2008), 55.
11. *Scratch*, directed by Doug Pray (Firewalks Film, 2001), DVD.

12. E-40, interview by author, April 5, 2007.
13. *Access Hollywood,* "Flavor Flav Going Back to School in New Show," October 1, 2009, http://www.today.com/id/33117640 /site/todayshow/ns/today-entertainment/t/flavor-flav-going -back-school-new-show/#.UQQinL9rjK0.
14. Shock G, interview by author, September 9, 2012.
15. "DVD Extras: Too Short interview," from *Something from Nothing: The Art of Rap,* directed by Ice-T and Andy Baybutt (London: Kaleidoscope Home Entertainment, 2012), DVD.
16. Matthew Kantor, "DJ Premier: Interview, Still the Owner," *Prefix Mag,* October 26, 2010, http://www.prefixmag.com /features/dj-premier/interview/45191/.
17. Joseph G. Schloss, *Making Beats: The Art of Sample-Based Hip-Hop* (Middletown, CT: Wesleyan University Press, 2004), 29.
18. Jim Fricke and Charlie Ahearn, *Yes Yes Y'all: The Experience Music Project Oral History of Hip-Hop's First Decade* (New York: Da Capo, 2002), 43.
19. Bill Adler, *Tougher Than Leather: The Rise of Run-DMC* (Los Angeles: Consafos Press, 2002), 21.
20. Ibid., 30.
21. Jim Fricke and Charlie Ahearn, *Yes Yes Y'all: The Experience Music Project Oral History of Hip-Hop's First Decade* (New York: Da Capo, 2002), 128.
22. Kool Moe Dee, *There's a God on the Mic: The True 50 Greatest MCs* (New York: Thunder's Mouth Press, 2003), 334–335, 339.
23. *Scratch,* directed by Doug Pray (Firewalks Film, 2001), DVD.
24. Jim Fricke and Charlie Ahearn, *Yes Yes Y'all: The Experience Music Project Oral History of Hip-Hop's First Decade* (New York: Da Capo, 2002), 63.
25. Patrick Jarenwattananon, "The Microphone Fiend on John Coltrane," NPR, November 23, 2009, http://www.npr.org /blogs/ablogsupreme/2009/11/rakim_on_john_coltrane.html.

26. Joseph G. Schloss, *Making Beats: The Art of Sample-Based Hip-Hop* (Middletown, CT: Wesleyan University Press, 2004), 30.

27. Andy Cat, interview by author, January 15, 2007.

28. Lateef, interview by author, May 17, 2007.

29. Vinnie Paz, interview by author, May 22, 2007.

30. HalftimeOnline, "Kool G Rap," November 12, 2003, http:// halftimeonline.net/portfolio/kool-g-rap/.

31. Steven Hager, "Coke La Rock: Hip Hop's First MC," Cannabis Cup video interview, September 12, 2010, https://www .youtube.com/watch?v=Hqi-_g894ss.

32. Richard Grabel, *NME* magazine, May 30, 1981, http://www .sleezyblue.com/funkyfour-nme.html.

33. David Ma, "The Kurtis Blow Interview," *Wax Poetics*, June 8, 2013, http://www.waxpoetics.com/features/articles/blessed -the-mic.

34. *Scratch,* directed by Doug Pray (Firewalks Film, 2001), DVD.

35. Jim Fricke and Charlie Ahearn, *Yes Yes Y'all: The Experience Music Project Oral History of Hip-Hop's First Decade* (New York: Da Capo, 2002), 79.

36. Big Daddy Kane, interview by author, March 31, 2008.

37. *Freestyle: The Art of Rhyme,* directed by Kevin Fitzgerald (Bowery Films, 2000), DVD.

38. Kool Moe Dee, *There's a God on the Mic: The True 50 Greatest MCs* (New York: Thunder's Mouth Press, 2003), 101, 23, 226.

39. Myka 9, interview by author, May 16, 2007.

40. Kool Moe Dee, *There's a God on the Mic: The True 50 Greatest MCs* (New York: Thunder's Mouth Press, 2003), 226, 306.

41. Sa'id, *BeatTips Manual: Some Insight on Producing Hip Hop–Rap Beats and Music,* fourth edition (New York: Superchamp Books, 2007), 258.

42. Prepare Yourself, "Digging the Music of Hiphop: These Are

the Standards Event," August 20, 2013, http://www.hiphop
archive.org/node/9577.

43. Brother J, interview by author, February 20, 2007.

44. Murs, interview by author, September 25, 2007.

45. *Something from Nothing: The Art of Rap*, directed by Ice-T and
Andy Baybutt (London: Kaleidoscope Home Entertain-
ment, 2012), DVD.

46. Pharoahe Monch, interview by author, May 20, 2008.

47. Lateef, interview by author, May 17, 2007.

48. Pharoahe Monch, interview by author, May 20, 2008.

49. Shock G, interview by author, October 3, 2007.

50. Planet Asia, interview by author, June 6, 2007.

51. Wise Intelligent, interview by author, June 1, 2007.

52. Zumbi, interview by author, May 3, 2007.

53. Esoteric, interview by author, August 31, 2012.

54. Royce Da 5′9″, interview by author, May 14, 2008.

55. Tech N9ne, interview by author, March 27, 2008.

56. Shock G, interview by author, October 3, 2007.

57. Del the Funky Homosapien, interview by author, October
14, 2007.

58. Adam Krims, *Rap Music and the Poetics of Identity* (Cambridge: Cambridge University Press, 2000), 59.

59. Paul Edwards, *How to Rap: The Art & Science of the Hip-Hop
MC* (Chicago: Chicago Review Press, 2009), 67.

60. Paul Edwards, *How to Rap 2: Advanced Flow and Delivery
Techniques* (Chicago: Chicago Review Press, 2013), xiii.

61. Kyle Adams, "On the Metrical Techniques of Flow in Rap
Music," *Music Theory Online: A Journal of Criticism, Commentary, Research, and Scholarship*, Volume 15, Number 5, October 2009, http://www.mtosmt.org/issues/mto.09.15.5/mto.09
.15.5.adams.html.

4. Influential Rappers

1. *Something from Nothing: The Art of Rap,* directed by Ice-T and Andy Baybutt (London: Kaleidoscope Home Entertainment, 2012), DVD.

2. Brian Coleman, *Check the Technique: Liner Notes for Hip-Hop Junkies* (New York: Villard, 2007), 202.

3. Kool G Rap, interview by author, October 30, 2007.

4. Kool Moe Dee, *There's a God on the Mic: The True 50 Greatest MCs* (New York: Thunder's Mouth Press, 2003), 334.

5. Jim Fricke and Charlie Ahearn, *Yes Yes Y'all: The Experience Music Project Oral History of Hip-Hop's First Decade* (New York: Da Capo, 2002), 74–75.

6. Chuck Jigsaw Creekmur, "Top 5 Dead or Alive: DJ Premier," Allhiphop.com, December 18, 2010, http://allhiphop.com /2010/12/18/top-5-dead-or-alive-dj-premier/.

7. Chairman Mao, "Rakim Interview," Redbull.com, 2013, http://www.redbullmusicacademy.com/lectures/rakim.

8. Chuck D, interview by author, June 10, 2008.

9. Chairman Mao, "Rakim Interview," Redbull.com, 2013, http://www.redbullmusicacademy.com/lectures/rakim.

10. Brian Coleman, *Check the Technique: Liner Notes for Hip-Hop Junkies* (New York: Villard, 2007), 202.

11. Jim Fricke and Charlie Ahearn, *Yes Yes Y'all: The Experience Music Project Oral History of Hip-Hop's First Decade* (New York: Da Capo, 2002), 265.

12. Big Daddy Kane, interview by author, March 31, 2008.

13. Robbie Ettelson, "Percee P—The Unkut Interview," Unkut .com, December 11, 2007, http://www.unkut.com/2007/12 /percee-p-the-unkut-interview/.

14. Chairman Mao, "Rakim Interview," Redbull.com, 2013, http://www.redbullmusicacademy.com/lectures/rakim.

15. Troy L. Smith, "DJ Easy Lee Interview," The Foundation, summer 2005, http://www.thafoundation.com/easylee.htm.

16. Chuck Jigsaw Creekmur, "Top 5 Dead or Alive: DJ Premier," Allhiphop.com, December 18, 2010, http://allhiphop .com/2010/12/18/top-5-dead-or-alive-dj-premier/.

17. Redbull.com, "Take Five: Pete Rock," August 26, 2011, http://www.redbull.com/cs/Satellite/en_US/Article/Take -Five-Pete-Rock-021243074516229.

18. Chairman Mao, "Rakim Interview," Redbull.com, 2013, http://www.redbullmusicacademy.com/lectures/rakim.

19. Kool Moe Dee, *There's a God on the Mic: The True 50 Greatest MCs* (New York: Thunder's Mouth Press, 2003), 292.

20. *The Show,* directed by Brian Robbins (Santa Monica, CA: Rysher Entertainment, 1995), DVD.

21. Big Daddy Kane, interview by author, March 31, 2008.

22. Brian Coleman, *Check the Technique: Liner Notes for Hip-Hop Junkies* (New York: Villard, 2007), 202.

23. Chairman Mao, "Rakim Interview," Redbull.com, 2013, http://www.redbullmusicacademy.com/lectures/rakim.

24. Rock, interview by author, May 29, 2007.

25. Tajal, interview by author, April 10, 2008.

26. Rah Digga, interview by author, May 6, 2008.

27. The RZA, *The Wu-Tang Manual* (New York: Penguin, 2005), 8–9.

28. Alvin "Aqua" Blanco, "Top 5 Dead or Alive: RZA," Allhip hop.com, January 22, 2009, http://allhiphop.com/2009/01 /22/top-5-dead-or-alive-rza/.

29. Havoc, interview by author, November 7, 2007.

30. MC Serch, interview by author, February 1, 2007.

31. Big Daddy Kane, interview by author, March 31, 2008.

32. Kool G Rap, interview by author, October 30, 2007.

33. Brian Coleman, *Check the Technique: Liner Notes for Hip-Hop Junkies* (New York: Villard, 2007), 204.

34. Kool Moe Dee, *There's a God on the Mic: The True 50 Greatest MCs* (New York: Thunder's Mouth Press, 2003), 324–325.
35. HalftimeOnline, "Rakim," May 10, 2006, http://halftime online.net/portfolio/rakim/.
36. Masta Ace, interview by author, April 24, 2007.
37. HalftimeOnline, "Rakim," May 10, 2006, http://halftime online.net/portfolio/rakim/.
38. Jay-Z, *Decoded* (New York: Spiegel & Grau, 2010), 16.
39. Michael A. Gonzales, "The Resurrection: Rakim," *Ego Trip Magazine,* 1997, http://www.egotripland.com/rakim_interview _ego_trip/.
40. Werner Von Wallenrod, "Competive Spirit—Kool G Rap Interview," *Werner von Wallenrod's Humble, Little Hip-Hop Blog,* May 1, 2011, http://wernervonwallenrod.blogspot.com /2011/05/competive-spirit-kool-g-rap-interview.html.
41. Grandmaster Flash and David Ritz, *The Adventures of Grand-master Flash: My Life, My Beats* (New York: Broadway Books, 2008), 216.
42. Kool Moe Dee, *There's a God on the Mic: The True 50 Greatest MCs* (New York: Thunder's Mouth Press, 2003), 226.
43. Insanul Ahmed, "Nas' 25 Favorite Albums," Complex.com, May 22, 2012, http://www.complex.com/music/2012/05/nas -25-favorite-albums/kool-g-rap-dj-polo-wanted-dead-or -alive.
44. Kool G Rap, interview by author, October 30, 2007.
45. Termanology, interview by author, February 5, 2007.
46. Diane Shabazz Varnie, "Top 5 Dead or Alive: Raekwon," Allhiphop.com, December 22, 2009, http://allhiphop.com /2009/12/22/top-5-dead-or-alive-raekwon/.
47. HalftimeOnline, "Kool G," November 12, 2003, http:// halftimeonline.net/portfolio/kool-g-rap/.
48. HalftimeOnline, "Big Daddy Kane," March 17, 2004, http:// halftimeonline.net/portfolio/big-daddy-kane/.

49. Jay-Z, *Decoded* (New York: Spiegel & Grau, 2010), 38.
50. Alvin "Aqua" Blanco, "Top 5 Dead or Alive: RZA," Allhip hop.com, January 22, 2009, http://allhiphop.com/2009/01 /22/top-5-dead-or-alive-rza/.
51. MTV.com, "The Greatest MCs of All Time," March 3, 2013, http://www.mtv.com/bands/h/hip_hop_week/2006/emcees /index5.jhtml.
52. O.C., interview by author, April 6, 2007.
53. Grandmaster Flash and David Ritz, *The Adventures of Grandmaster Flash: My Life, My Beats* (New York: Broadway Books, 2008), 215.
54. Kool Moe Dee, *There's a God on the Mic: The True 50 Greatest MCs* (New York: Thunder's Mouth Press, 2003), 318.
55. MTV.com, "The Greatest MCs of All Time," March 3, 2013, http://www.mtv.com/bands/h/hip_hop_week/2006/emcees /index6.jhtml.

5. Influential Beatmakers

1. Sean Price, interview by author, May 18, 2007.
2. Brother Ali, interview by author, June 20, 2007.
3. Yukmouth, interview by author, February 21, 2007.
4. Egotripland.com, "Da Beatminerz's 10 Favorite Sample Flips," October 1, 2012, http://www.egotripland.com/gallery/da -beatminerz-10-favorite-sample-flips/9-main-source-just -hangin-out-remix-wild-pitch-1991/.
5. Sa'id, *BeatTips Manual: Some Insight on Producing Hip Hop-Rap Beats and Music,* fourth edition (New York: Superchamp Books, 2007), 258.
6. Jazz FM, "Exclusive: Sugar Hill—a legend speaks!" July 19, 2010, http://www.jazzfm.com/2010/07/exclusive-sugar-hill -records-a-legend-speaks/.
7. JayQuan, "Get Funky, Make Money & Ya Don't Stop: The Story of Duke Bootee aka Ed Fletcher," The Foundation,

February 2010, http://www.thafoundation.com/dukebootee.htm.

8. Chuck Jigsaw Creekmur, "Top 5 Dead or Alive Producers: DJ Premier," Allhiphop.com, May 27, 2009, http://allhiphop.com/2009/05/27/top-5-dead-or-alive-producers-dj-premier/.

9. Keith Murphy, "DMC Says 'Larry Smith's Musical Arsenal Equals Dr. Dre's,'" Vibe.com, April 14, 2010, http://www.vibe.com/article/dmc-says-larry-smiths-musical-arsenal-equals-dr-dres.

10. Chuck Jigsaw Creekmur, "Mannie Fresh: Top 5 Dead or Alive Producers," Allhiphop.com, July 28, 2010, http://allhiphop.com/2010/07/28/mannie-fresh-top-5-dead-or-alive-producers/.

11. Brian Coleman, *Rakim Told Me: Wax Facts Straight from the Original Artists—The '80s* (Somerville, MA: Wax Facts, 2005), 141.

12. *Ego Trip Magazine*, "Da Beatminerz's 10 Favorite Sample Flips," October 5, 2011, http://www.egotripland.com/da-beatminerz-10-favorite-sample-flips/.

13. *Beat Kings: The History of Hip Hop*, directed by Beat Kings (Brooklyn, NY: Nature Sounds, 2006), DVD.

14. Chuck Jigsaw Creekmur, "Top 5 Dead or Alive Producers: DJ Premier," Allhiphop.com, May 27, 2009, http://allhiphop.com/2009/05/27/top-5-dead-or-alive-producers-dj-premier/.

15. Dave Tompkins, "Return to the World as a Thought," *Crunkster*, August 5, 2004, http://crunkster.abstractdynamics.org/archives/003807.html.

16. Ibid.

17. Ibid.

18. Noah Callahan-Bever, "Large Professor Feature for XXL," *ncb1979*, August 30, 2010, http://ncb1979.com/2010/08/30/large-professor-feature-for-xxl-march-2002/.

19. *Ego Trip Magazine*, "Large Professor's 10 Favorite Sample

Flips," January 17, 2012, http://www.egotripland.com/large
-professor-sample-flips/2/.

20. Angus Batey, "Ultramagnetic MC's—Critical Beatdown: An
Oral History," Angus Batey.com, July 16, 2013, http://www
.angusbatey.com/index.php?id=589&category=features.

21. Dave Tompkins, "Return to the World as a Thought," *Crunkster,* August 5, 2004, http://crunkster.abstractdynamics.org
/archives/003807.html.

22. Robbie Ettelson, "Large Pro—The Unkut Interview," Unkut
.com, April 13, 2009, http://www.unkut.com/2009/04/large
-pro-the-unkut-interview/.

23. Chuck Jigsaw Creekmur, "Top 5 Dead or Alive: Domingo,"
Allhiphop.com, February 10, 2009, http://allhiphop.com
/2009/02/10/top-5-dead-or-alive-producers-domingo/.

24. Lev Harris, "The Quietus, Baker's Dozen: UNKLE'S James
Lavelle On His 13 Favourite Records," *The Quietus,* April
20, 2011, http://thequietus.com/articles/06129-james-lavelle
-unkle-favourite-records?page=6.

25. Kembrew McLeod, "How Copyright Law Changed Hip
Hop: An interview with Public Enemy's Chuck D and Hank
Shocklee," *Stay Free! Magazine,* issue 20, http://www.stay
freemagazine.org/archives/20/public_enemy.html.

26. Ibid.

27. Mike Diver, "The Beastie Boys—Interview Preview," *Clash,*
October 7, 2009, http://www.clashmusic.com/feature/the
-beastie-boys-interview-preview.

28. Veronica Fox, "Hank Shocklee vs. Jason Forrest," *XLR8R
Magazine,* September 19, 2005, http://www.xlr8r.com/fea
tures/2005/08/hank-shocklee-jason-forrest-shoc.

29. Ibid.

30. Ibid.

31. Ibid.

32. DJ Sorce-1, "From The Soul: The Music and Influence of De

La (Part One)," *The Smoking Section*, August 19, 2008, http://
smokingsection.uproxx.com/TSS/2008/08/from-the-soul
-the-music-and-influence-of-de-la-part-one#ixzz2Iju
RoLP4.

33. Brian Coleman, *Check the Technique: Liner Notes for Hip-Hop
Junkies* (New York: Villard, 2007), 144.

34. DJ Sorce-1, "Reconstructing the De La Soul Years with Prince
Paul (Part Two)," *The Smoking Section*, August 21, 2008, http://
smokingsection.uproxx.com/TSS/2008/08/reconstructing
-the-de-la-soul-years-with-prince-paul-part-two.

35. The RZA, *The Wu-Tang Manual* (New York: Penguin, 2005),
190.

36. Brian Coleman, *Check the Technique: Liner Notes for Hip-Hop
Junkies* (New York: Villard, 2007), 148.

37. DJ Sorce-1, "Reconstructing the De La Soul Years with Prince
Paul (Part Two)," *The Smoking Section*, August 21, 2008, http://
smokingsection.uproxx.com/TSS/2008/08/reconstructing
-the-de-la-soul-years-with-prince-paul-part-two.

38. Lev Harris, "The Quietus, Baker's Dozen: UNKLE'S James
Lavelle On His 13 Favourite Records," *The Quietus*, April 20,
2011, http://thequietus.com/articles/06129-james-lavelle-un
kle-favourite-records?page=7.

6. Hip-Hop Instruments

1. The RZA, *The Wu-Tang Manual* (New York: Penguin, 2005),
191–192.

2. Akai Professional, "Interview with the Alchemist," http://
www.akaipro.com/content208227.

3. Andy Cat, interview by author, March 10, 2013.

4. Brother Ali, interview by author, June 20, 2007.

5. Alexa Camp, "Interview: Rahzel," *Slant Magazine*, July 21,
2006, http://www.slantmagazine.com/features/article/inter
view-rahzel.

6. *Fat Lace Magazine,* "Doug E. Fresh Interview," May 23, 2013, http://fatlacemagazine.com/2008/10/doug-e-fresh-interview/.

7. Prepare Yourself, "Digging the Music of Hiphop: These Are the Standards Event Video," August 20, 2013, http://www .hiphoparchive.org/node/9577.

8. Ibid.

9. Ibid.

10. The RZA, *The Wu-Tang Manual* (New York: Penguin, 2005), 190.

11. Robbie Ettelson, "Large Pro—The Unkut Interview," Unkut .com, April 13 2009, http://www.unkut.com/2009/04/large -pro-the-unkut-interview/.

12. Billy Jam, "Creator of the Scratch: Grand Wizard Theodore," HipHop Slam, July 14, 2013, http://www.hiphopslam.com /articles/int_grandwizardtheo.html.

13. Paul Tingen, "DJ Premier, Hip-Hop Producer," *Sound On Sound,* July 2007, http://www.soundonsound.com/sos/jul07 /articles/djpremier.htm.

14. Andre Torres, "The Architect," *Scratch Magazine,* summer 2004, issue 1, p. 78.

15. Riot Sound, "DJ Revolution: King of the Decks," June 7, 2013, http://www.riotsound.com/hip-hop/rap/interviews /DJ-Revolution/index.php.

16. Ibid.

17. Billy Jam, "Creator of the Scratch: Grand Wizard Theodore," HipHop Slam, http://www.hiphopslam.com/articles/int_grand wizardtheo.html.

18. Andrew Friedman, "Pete Rock: The Creator," Guitar Center, July 9, 2013, http://gc.guitarcenter.com/interview/peterock/.

19. Ken Micallef, "Respect: Kurtis Mantronik," *Electronic Musician,* June 1, 2008, http://www.emusician.com/news/0766 /respect-kurtis-mantronik/142729.

20. Brian Coleman, *Check the Technique: Liner Notes for Hip-Hop Junkies* (New York: Villard, 2007), 414.

21. Ibid., 38.

22. Ibid., 206.

23. Ibid., 443.

24. JNOTA, "Buckwild Interview from SP-1200," *The Lost Tapes*, May 4, 2013, http://claaa7.blogspot.co.uk/2011/08/buckwild -interview-from-sp1200.html.

25. Ben Detrick, "The Dirty Heartbeat of the Golden Age: Reminiscing on the SP-1200, the Machine That Defined New York Hip-Hop," *The Village Voice*, November 6, 2007, http:// www.villagevoice.com/2007-11-06/music/the-dirty-heartbeat -of-the-golden-age/.

26. Sa'id, *BeatTips Manual: Some Insight on Producing Hip Hop-Rap Beats and Music*, fourth edition (New York: Superchamp Books, 2007), 200.

27. Daniel Isenberg, "DJ Muggs Tells All: The Stories Behind His Classic Records (Part 1)," Complex.com, January 26, 2013, http://www.complex.com/music/2013/01/dj-muggs -tells-all-the-stories-behind-his-classic-records-part-1/house -of-pain-jump-around.

28. Ben Detrick, "The Dirty Heartbeat of the Golden Age: Reminiscing on the SP-1200, the Machine That Defined New York Hip-Hop," *The Village Voice*, November 6, 2007, http:// www.villagevoice.com/2007-11-06/music/the-dirty-heart beat-of-the-golden-age/.

29. JNOTA "Buckwild Interview from SP-1200," *The Lost Tapes*, May 4, 2013, http://claaa7.blogspot.co.uk/2011/08/buckwild -interview-from-sp1200.html.

30. Ben Detrick, "The Dirty Heartbeat of the Golden Age: Reminiscing on the SP-1200, the Machine That Defined New York Hip-Hop," *The Village Voice*, November 6, 2007, http://

www.villagevoice.com/2007-11-06/music/the-dirty-heart beat-of-the-golden-age/.

31. Akai Professional, "Interview with the Alchemist," June 2, 2013, http://www.akaipro.com/artist/alchemist.

32. Paul Tingen, "DJ Premier, Hip-Hop Producer," *Sound On Sound*, July 2007, http://www.soundonsound.com/sos/jul07 /articles/djpremier.htm.

33. Andre Torres, "The Architect," *Scratch Magazine*, summer 2004, issue 1, p. 76.

34. Paul Tingen, "DJ Premier, Hip-Hop Producer," *Sound On Sound*, July 2007, http://www.soundonsound.com/sos/jul07 /articles/djpremier.htm.

35. Akai Professional, "Interview with the Alchemist," June 2, 2013, http://www.akaipro.com/artist/alchemist.

36. Richard Buskin, "Afrika Bambaataa & The Soulsonic Force: 'Planet Rock,'" *Sound On Sound*, November 2008, http:// www.soundonsound.com/sos/nov08/articles/classictracks _1108.htm.

37. Andre Torres, "The Architect," *Scratch Magazine*, summer 2004, issue 1, p. 76.

38. The RZA, *The Wu-Tang Manual* (New York: Penguin, 2005), 199.

7. Old School/New School

1. Grandmaster Flash and David Ritz, *The Adventures of Grandmaster Flash: My Life, My Beats* (New York: Broadway Books, 2008), 47.

2. Jim Fricke and Charlie Ahearn, *Yes Yes Y'all: The Experience Music Project Oral History of Hip-Hop's First Decade* (New York: Da Capo, 2002), 46.

3. David Toop, *Rap Attack, No. 3: African Rap to Global Hip Hop* (London: Serpent's Tail, 2000), 66.

4. Grandmaster Flash and David Ritz, *The Adventures of Grand-*

master Flash: My Life, My Beats (New York: Broadway Books, 2008), 53.

5. Ibid., 75.

6. Jim Fricke and Charlie Ahearn, *Yes Yes Y'all: The Experience Music Project Oral History of Hip-Hop's First Decade* (New York: Da Capo, 2002), 59.

7. Ibid., 63.

8. Mark Skillz, "Cheeba, Cheeba Y'all!" *Wax Poetics*, August 23, 2013, http://hiphop101a.blogspot.co.uk/2007/09/cheeba-cheeba-yall.html.

9. Steven J. Horowitz, "Prodigy Explains Why He Respects Waka Flocka Flame & Soulja Boy," *HipHopbx*, May 31, 2011, http://www.hiphopdx.com/index/news/id.15354/title.prodigy-explains-why-he-respects-waka-flocka-flame-soulja-boy.

10. Kool G Rap, interview by author, October 30, 2007.

11. Jim Fricke and Charlie Ahearn, *Yes Yes Y'all: The Experience Music Project Oral History of Hip-Hop's First Decade* (New York: Da Capo, 2002), 212.

12. Jazz FM, "Exclusive: Sugar Hill—a legend speaks!" July 19, 2010, http://www.jazzfm.com/2010/07/exclusive-sugar-hill-records-a-legend-speaks/.

13. Jim Fricke and Charlie Ahearn, *Yes Yes Y'all: The Experience Music Project Oral History of Hip-Hop's First Decade* (New York: Da Capo, 2002), 328.

14. Ibid.

15. Rob Marriott, "Interview: Rakim Talks about the Making of 'Follow The Leader,'" Complex.com, July 26, 2013, http://www.complex.com/music/2013/07/rakim-follow-the-leader-interview/page/2.

16. JayQuan, "Grandmaster Mele Mel Interview," The Foundation, 2005 http://www.thafoundation.com/melemelintf5.htm.

17. Louis Romain, "Riding Off the Deep End," *The Source* magazine, October 1993, p. 48.

18. T3, interview by author, January 31, 2007.

19. Bill Adler, *Tougher Than Leather: The Rise of Run-DMC* (Los Angeles: Consafos Press, 2002), ix.

20. Jim Fricke and Charlie Ahearn, *Yes Yes Y'all: The Experience Music Project Oral History of Hip-Hop's First Decade* (New York: Da Capo, 2002), 328.

21. *The Show,* directed by Brian Robbins (Santa Monica, CA: Rysher Entertainment, 1995), DVD.

22. Bill Adler, *Tougher Than Leather: The Rise of Run-DMC* (Los Angeles: Consafos Press, 2002), 56–57.

23. Jazz FM, "Exclusive: Sugar Hill—a legend speaks!" July 19, 2010, http://www.jazzfm.com/2010/07/exclusive-sugar-hill-records-a-legend-speaks/.

24. Jim Fricke and Charlie Ahearn, *Yes Yes Y'all: The Experience Music Project Oral History of Hip-Hop's First Decade* (New York: Da Capo, 2002), 327.

25. Bill Adler, *Tougher Than Leather: The Rise of Run-DMC* (Los Angeles: Consafos Press, 2002), 80.

26. Ibid., 81.

27. HalftimeOnline, "Mele Mel," March 11, 2013, http://halftimeonline.net/mele-mel/.

28. Bill Adler, *Tougher Than Leather: The Rise of Run-DMC* (Los Angeles: Consafos Press, 2002), 80.

29. Rob Marriott, "Interview: Rakim Talks about the Making of 'Follow The Leader,'" Complex.com, July 26, 2013, http://www.complex.com/music/2013/07/rakim-follow-the-leader-interview/page/2.

30. Bill Adler, *Tougher Than Leather: The Rise of Run-DMC* (Los Angeles: Consafos Press, 2002), ix.

31. The RZA, *The Wu-Tang Manual* (New York: Penguin, 2005), 238.

32. Louis Romain, "Riding Off the Deep End," *The Source* magazine, October 1993, p. 48.

8. The Golden Age of Hip-Hop

1. *Oxford Dictionaries*, s.v. "golden age," February 6, 2013, http://oxforddictionaries.com/us/definition/american-english/golden -age.
2. Andrew J. Rausch, *I Am Hip-Hop: Conversations on the Music and Culture* (Lanham, MD: Scarecrow, 2011), 197–198.
3. McSerch, interview by author, February 1, 2007.
4. Phife, interview by author, February 17, 2007.
5. Brother Ali, interview by author, June 20, 2007.
6. Zumbi, interview by author, May 3, 2007.
7. Fredro Starr, interview by author, October 1, 2007.
8. T3, interview by author, January 31, 2007.
9. Steven J. Horowitz, "Prodigy Explains Why He Respects Waka Flocka Flame & Soulja Boy," *HipHopDX*, May 31, 2011, http://www.hiphopdx.com/index/news/id.15354/title .prodigy-explains-why-he-respects-waka-flocka-flame -soulja-boy.
10. Brother J, interview by author, February 20, 2007.
11. Gift of Gab, interview by author, September 20, 2007.
12. T3, interview by author, January 31, 2007.
13. Mike Diver, "The Beastie Boys—Interview Preview," *Clash*, October 7, 2009, http://www.clashmusic.com/feature/the -beastie-boys-interview-preview.
14. Nelson George, "Hip-Hop's Founding Fathers Speak the Truth," in *That's the Joint!: The Hip-Hop Studies Reader*, eds. Murray Forman and Mark Anthony Neal (New York: Routledge, 2004), 50.
15. Dan LeRoy, *Paul's Boutique* (New York: Continuum, 2006), 47.
16. Tech N9ne, interview by author, March 27, 2008.
17. R.A. the Rugged Man, interview by author, May 8, 2007.
18. Papoose, interview by author, July 2, 2007.

19. MC Serch, interview by author, February 1, 2007.
20. Andrew J. Rausch, *I Am Hip-Hop: Conversations on the Music and Culture* (Lanham, MD: Scarecrow, 2011), 198.
21. Sha'Linda Jeanine, "Camp Lo & Pete Rock: Time Machine," *HipHopDX*, May 31, 2011, http://www.hiphopdx .com/index/interviews/id.1708/title.camp-lo-pete-rock-time -machine.
22. Pharoahe Monch, interview by author, May 20, 2008.
23. Kool G Rap, interview by author, October 30, 2007.
24. Myka 9, interview by author, May 16, 2007.
25. Paul W. Arnold, "Cee-Lo Green: What A Long, Strange Trip It's Been," *HipHopDX*, May 20, 2008, http://www.hip hopdx.com/index/interviews/id.1124/title.cee-lo-green -what-a-long-strange-trip-its-been.
26. AZ, interview by author, March 21, 2007.
27. Vinnie Paz, interview by author, May 22, 2007.
28. Jake Paine, "Hank Shocklee: Instant Vintage," *HipHopDX*, November 6, 2007, http://www.hiphopdx.com/index/inter views/id.919/title.hank-shocklee-instant-vintage.
29. Pigeon John, interview by author, May 7, 2007.
30. Chuck D, interview by author, June 10, 2008.
31. Kool G Rap, interview by author, October 30, 2007.
32. Pigeon John, interview by author, May 7, 2007.
33. Bobby Creekwater, interview by author, June 15, 2007.
34. R.A. the Rugged Man, interview by author, May 8, 2007.
35. Termanology, interview by author, February 5, 2007.
36. HalftimeOnline, "GZA (Wu-Tang)," April 10, 2006, http:// halftimeonline.net/portfolio/gza-wu-tang/.
37. Dan LeRoy, *Paul's Boutique* (New York: Continuum, 2006), 47.
38. Brian Coleman, *Check the Technique: Liner Notes for Hip-Hop Junkies* (New York: Villard, 2007), 153.
39. Reginald C. Dennis, "Code of Silence," *The Source* magazine, January 1993, p. 39.

9. Landmark Albums in Hip-Hop History

1. Darren Ressler, "Charlie Ahearn—Director of Wild Style (Interview)," *New York Beat,* May, 19 2011, http://newyork beatandfilm.wordpress.com/category/charlie-ahearn-director -of-wild-style-interview/.

2. Charlie Ahearn, *Wild Style: The Sampler* (New York: power-House Books, 2007), 207.

3. Ibid., 83.

4. Ibid., 193.

5. Troy L. Smith, "Fab 5 Freddy Interview," The Foundation, 2005, http://www.thafoundation.com/Fab.htm.

6. Charlie Ahearn, *Wild Style: The Sampler* (New York: power-House Books, 2007), 2.

7. Bill Adler, *Tougher Than Leather: The Rise of Run-DMC* (Los Angeles: Consafos Press, 2002), 89.

8. Ibid., 91.

9. Ibid.

10. Kool Moe Dee, *There's a God on the Mic: The True 50 Greatest MCs* (New York: Thunder's Mouth Press, 2003), 111, 112, 113.

11. MTV.com, "The Greatest MCs of All Time," March 3, 2013, http://www.mtv.com/bands/h/hip_hop_week/2006/emcees /index8.jhtml.

12. Insanul Ahmed, "Nas' 25 Favorite Albums," Complex.com, May 22, 2012, http://www.complex.com/music/2012/05/nas -25-favorite-albums/eric-b-rakim-paid-in-full.

13. Chuck Jigsaw Creekmur, "Rakim: The Lost Interview," All-hiphop.com, April 30, 2009, http://allhiphop.com/2009/04 /30/rakim-the-lost-interview/.

14. Martin A. Berrios, "Class Of '88: Paid In Full," Allhiphop .com, February 29, 2008, http://allhiphop.com/2008/02/29 /class-of-88-paid-in-full/.

15. Chairman Mao, "Behind the Boards: The Legacy of Marley Marl," *Ego Trip Magazine,* January 4, 2012, http://www .egotripland.com/marley-marl-interview-ego-trip-maga zine/2/.

16. Kool Moe Dee, *There's a God on the Mic: The True 50 Greatest MCs* (New York: Thunder's Mouth Press, 2003), 271–274.

17. Chuck Jigsaw Creekmur, "Top 5 Dead or Alive: Ice Cube," Allhiphop.com, June 8, 2010, http://allhiphop.com/2010/06 /08/top-5-dead-or-alive-ice-cube/.

18. Antonino D'Ambrosio, "Interview: Chuck D," *The Progressive,* August 2005, http://progressive.org/mag_chuckd.

19. Sherron Shabazz, "A Conversation with Chuck D," *The Real Hip-Hop,* April 11, 2013, http://therealhip-hop.com/?p=162.

20. Insanul Ahmed, "Nas' 25 Favorite Albums," Complex.com, May 22, 2012, http://www.complex.com/music/2012/05/nas -25-favorite-albums/public-enemy-it-takes-a-nation-of-mil lions-to-hold-us-back.

21. Lev Harris, "The Quietus, Baker's Dozen: UNKLE'S James Lavelle On His 13 Favourite Records," *The Quietus,* April 20, 2011, http://thequietus.com/articles/06129-james-lavelle -unkle-favourite-records?page=5.

22. Andrew J. Rausch, *I Am Hip-Hop: Conversations on the Music and Culture* (Lanham, MD: Scarecrow, 2011), 15.

23. Murs, interview by author, September 25, 2007.

24. Andrew Romano, "Rick Rubin on Crashing Kanye's Album in 15 Days," *The Daily Beast,* June 27, 2013, http://www.the dailybeast.com/newsweek/2013/06/26/rick-rubin-on-crash ing-kanye-s-album-in-15-days.html?src=longreads.

25. *The Show,* directed by Brian Robbins (Santa Monica, CA: Rysher Entertainment, 1995), DVD.

26. Andrew J. Rausch, *I Am Hip-Hop: Conversations on the Music and Culture* (Lanham, MD: Scarecrow, 2011), 96.

27. Mike Diver, "The Beastie Boys—Interview Preview," *Clash*, October 7, 2009, http://www.clashmusic.com/feature/the -beastie-boys-interview-preview.

28. Dan LeRoy, *Paul's Boutique* (New York: Continuum, 2006), 21.

29. Paul Tingen, "The Dust Brothers: Sampling, Remixing & The Boat Studio," *Sound On Sound*, May 2005, http://www .soundonsound.com/sos/may05/articles/dust.htm.

30. Ibid.

31. Dan LeRoy, *Paul's Boutique* (New York: Continuum, 2006), 22.

32. Nancy Whalen, "Gathering Dust," *Bay Area Music Magazine*, April 6, 1994.

33. Dan LeRoy, *Paul's Boutique* (New York: Continuum, 2006), 78.

34. Ibid., 84.

35. Ibid., 63.

36. Carl Jacobson, "Bob Power PRO/FILE," *Electronic Musician*, October 1, 2011, http://www.emusician.com/engineers -producers/0989/bob-power-pro/file/143440.

37. Insanul Ahmed, "Nas' 25 Favorite Albums," Complex.com, May 22, 2012, http://www.complex.com/music/2012/05/nas -25-favorite-albums/a-tribe-called-quest-the-low-end-theory.

38. Brian Coleman, *Check the Technique: Liner Notes for Hip-Hop Junkies* (New York: Villard, 2007), 447.

39. *Ego Trip Land*, "Prince Paul's 10 Favorite Sample Flips," July 13, 2011, http://www.egotripland.com/gallery/prince-pauls -10-favorite-sample-flips/6-tribe-called-quest-verses-from -the-abstract-jive-1991/.

40. Carl Jacobson, "Bob Power PRO/FILE," *Electronic Musician*, October 1, 2011, http://www.emusician.com/engineers-pro ducers/0989/bob-power-pro/file/143440.

41. *Ego Trip Land,* "Da Beatminerz's 10 Favorite Sample Flips," October 1, 2012, http://www.egotripland.com/gallery/da -beatminerz-10-favorite-sample-flips/7-a-tribe-called-quest -skypager-jive-1991/.
42. Carl Jacobson, "Bob Power PRO/FILE," *Electronic Musician,* October 1, 2011, http://www.emusician.com/engineers-pro ducers/0989/bob-power-pro/file/143440.

Index